Finding Fletcher

Lance Patterson

John 3:30

By Lance Patterson

ISBN-13: 978-1987739213
ISBN-10: 1987739213

To my wife, Leah:

who has been by my side through it all
and without whom this story would not
be possible.

Table of Contents

Chapter One
Mt. Pinatubo

The dark blue waters of the South China Sea glimmering in the morning sun reached to the lighter sky blue where they blended on the horizon. Some days it was hard to tell where one ended and the other began. We were behind a KC-10 Air Force tanker, about to take on fuel before starting a bombing run on the Crow Valley range west of Clark Air Base in the Philippines.

I nudged the throttle of my A-4E Skyhawk slightly forward trying to urge the fuel probe into the large basket on the end of a fuel hose extending from a boom behind the tail of the tanker. The KC-10 was usually easier to plug than the Marine KC-130 that we more often used because the receptacle basket was larger and heavier, and more stable in the wind. The KC-10 used a boom that an operator guided down from the back of the plane to plug into Air Force fighters, but they adapted it for Navy/Marine aircraft by adding an eleven-foot hose and a large basket.

Once connected the basket had to be pushed forward at least five feet to start the fuel flow. This created a loop in the hose and left only six feet of space from the end of the fuel probe to the boom. The A-4E probe extended out to the right side of the nose cone so that when plugged the basket was beside the aircraft and when pushed in there was only three to four feet separating the nose and the boom. It took a steady hand on the stick and the throttle, especially when the airflow would catch the loop in the hose and whip it over to slap the nose cone of the Skyhawk.

The A-4 had a long distinguished history. Introduced in 1954, it was designed with tall landing gear to carry one atom bomb which it would release as it climbed into a pop-up delivery, a loop to lob the bomb at its target while the A-4 dived for the ground to get away as quick as possible. It was essentially a suicide mission. With the entry of the B-52 into the service the A-4 mission was changed to a light attack, close air support (CAS) bomber, and was used extensively by the U.S. Navy in the Vietnam War.

An A-4 flown by Lt. Everett Alvarez, Jr. in 1964, was the first U.S. aircraft shot down over North Vietnam. The A-4 also has the distinction of being the only aircraft to ever shoot down an enemy fighter with a Zuni rocket. As the Vietnam War came to an end and a new generation of fighter aircraft came on line the A-4 was relegated to support and training roles. It turned out, although it was underpowered, to be a not too bad fighter and was the first aircraft used by the Navy Fighter Weapon's School at TOPGUN. At VC-5 in the Philippines we used them in a variety of roles including towing banners and drones, flying missile profiles against ship radar defenses, dropping bombs and flying air combat as adversaries for fleet exercises in the West Pacific.

In early April 1991, I was flying wing on John "Horse" Cochrane. Horse and I had a contest going to see who could make the most plugs on a tanker without a miss. I eventually won with seventeen straight plugs beating him by one, but by the end of the tour he had one more total plug than I did. On this morning the matter had not yet been settled. Horse had already taken on fuel. I couldn't afford to miss.

The tanker was flying a racetrack pattern over Scarborough Shoals about a hundred fifty miles west of Subic Bay. I was behind the basket moving in to plug when the big aircraft reached the end of its straight leg and banked into a left turn. The basket slid out away to my right and then up slightly as I followed in the turn. I tweaked the throttle back and maintained my position behind the basket until we came out of the turn, then gently pushed it forward, plugged and got my fuel.

COMEX (Commence Exercise) was at 0900 and we had about twenty minutes to get to our initial point well south of the tanker. The tanker track was at fifteen thousand feet but we intended to go in low and began a descent down to three thousand. We had an escort of F-18 Hornets flying above us and were supposed to have F-16s from Clark opposing us. At the start of the exercise we dropped to below one hundred feet over the water and started in toward the mountain range on the peninsula on the west side of Subic Bay. The Hornets apparently did their job, as we never did see an F-16.

The ridge on the peninsula was over 3,000 feet with some peaks close to 3,500. We hugged the water and then the slopes on the west side popping over the ridge and dropping down over Subic Bay heading to the northeast toward another mountain range with a peak in the middle called Mt. Pinatubo. Mt. Pinatubo is at the southern end of a ridge of mountains known as the Spine that runs up the west coast of Luzon from Subic Bay to the Lingayen Gulf.

We wanted to stay low as we left the bay and cross Lima Valley to a hump called the Saddle and then skirt across a remote jungle area that was so primitive it we called it Prehistoric Valley. The west side of Pinatubo dropped into a series of deep ravines separated by narrow ridges and covered with an impossibly thick carpet of lush green jungle. Flying over it you almost expected to see dinosaurs roaming around. From there we were going to pop up over the top of the Pinatubo ridge to descend on targets with twenty-five pound practice bombs, what we affectionately called "blue death" because of their color, in the Crow Valley range to the northeast.

As we came off the water there appeared to be low clouds or haze on the ground that was so thick that it greatly limited our visibility. We began a slow climb to stay in visual contact and then it became clear that haze was actually smoke. On the ground ash had fallen that was so white it looked like snow. We wound up coming in to Crow Valley more from the south than the west but as we crossed over Pinatubo we saw five plumes of smoke rising from vents at the base of the mountain on the west and northwest sides of the peak. They had just broken open within thirty minutes of our crossing and the tops of the ash clouds were at about three thousand feet. By afternoon the plumes had reached ten thousand.

We were barely able to see our target through the smoke, but when we picked it out we came in steep at a forty-five degree angle, pickled our loads and pulled out of the dive at around 2,000 feet, then popped up above the smoke into the clear air. We couldn't see our hits and got no report from the spotters because couldn't see them either. It turned out Horse and I were the first ones to see the beginning of the Mt. Pinatubo eruption, from the air at least.

Over the next two months the vents continued to blow ash, sometimes up to near twenty thousand feet. Other days were just minimal. Volcanologists were watching events closely from Clark Air Base. Clark was just ten miles to the east of Mt. Pinatubo. Cubi Point, the air field at the Subic Bay Naval Station, was twenty-one miles by the TACAN navigational beacon at the end of the runway to the south of the volcano. All of our flight exercises were planned to fly plenty clear of the volcanic vents.

In September 1990 I had proposed to the love of my life, Leah Dequina (affectionately called Lhey), and she accepted, but trying to set a date for the wedding had proved difficult. In October and November I was on detachments (dets) to Japan and South Korea. Then in January 1991 the Gulf War started and all Navy personnel were restricted to the base. At the beginning of February I was sent to TOPGUN for the adversary course, to learn Soviet strategy and techniques in order to provide a realistic air combat picture for the fleet to train with.

It was an honor to be chosen but TOPGUN turned out to be a personal disappointment. Since I wasn't stateside I didn't have my own plane to fly and had to depend on TOPGUN to provide one of their A-4s. The instructors were using F-16s, but they flew them so hard that they had found several cracked wing spars and a couple weeks before I arrived they were grounded. As a result there were no A-4s available for me to use. I went through the ground school and sat in on the debriefs. I was still an adversary pilot in the Philippines but because I missed the flight training I was unable to be an instructor. It was still a great experience. Afterward I took three weeks leave to travel across the country and visit family and friends before heading back.

It was a good time to be in the military and be home. I couldn't buy a meal anywhere. Everybody took care of me, and I wasn't even in the action. I had just returned to the Philippines near the end of March and our flight out to the tanker was only my second or third hop since arriving back in the Philippines.

There was a mountain of paperwork for the Navy, U.S. Immigrations, and the Philippine government, plus marriage counseling from the chaplaincy for both of us, for Lhey and I to get married. It would have been easier to get a fiancee visa, but then we would have had to wait another year and a half.

We had to attend a seminar on the base. A Nun spoke to the girls, and a Protestant chaplain, a woman no less, spoke to the men. She was foulmouthed and profane and absolutely insulting. What in the world can a single woman chaplain trying to act like one of the guys teach men about marriage? It's no wonder sailors were so wild when considering the lack of moral leadership we had.

Lhey had to attend a Bride's School for four days on the base. When I asked her what she had learned she said, "How to get your money!" One day one of the lecturers was late so the other girls told Lhey to teach the class. She had already become a leader among them because of her command of English. She was the only one of 21 girls who had been to college. Chances are she was the only one who wasn't a bargirl either. She asked them if they wanted her to teach them how to go to heaven. They said yes, and she shared the gospel with them.

We finally had enough of the checks in the block to try and decide on a date. And then it happened.

Seismologists began measuring earthquakes, which were almost daily, although relatively small. But the tremors began to build and on June 10, the Air Force evacuated all but essential personnel and flew all of their aircraft away from Clark Air Base. A line of cars miles long wound slowly along the zigzag, the nickname of the old National Highway, that twisted its way via a series of hairpin turns over the low mountain ranges east of Olongapo City at Subic Bay to San Fernando north of Manila, and further north to Angeles City where Clark was located.

The squadron had sent two airplanes to Okinawa on June 11 and scheduled six more for June 12 to establish a det so we could hold an exercise with the USS Abraham Lincoln in the event Cubi Point was shut down due to the volcano. Eight pilots were ready to fly four A-4Es (single seat) and two TA-4Js (two seats) away. I was leading one flight and Horse the other. We had packed light travel bags thinking we wouldn't be gone long for a 0830 brief and 1000 launch time.

At 0905 we were walking out of the large VC-5 hangar bay when one of my wingmen, Lt. Jude Stafford, grabbed my shoulder and said, "Look," pointing across the runway to the north. A massive gray cloud was billowing up through about ten thousand feet. I had a camera on my shoulder and snapped a few pictures and then ran to plane, did the fastest pre-flight inspection on record, closed all the panels and climbed into the cockpit. While waiting for a start cart I took some more pictures at 0915. The ash cloud continued to climb to about 20,000 feet and began to mushroom to the west and south, turning darker as it spread until the leading edge of it of was resting on the northern end of Subic Bay.

We reached the hold short before the runway just as a Quantas DC-10 took off. Because of the unstable air from the airliner's jet wash we had to wait five minutes before we could take off. We were cleared to "posit and hold" on the runway but all we could do was sit and wait. The dark, churning cloud had turned black over the bay and was rolling over the water right at us. The tops had already spread and covered the bay blocking out the sun.

After what seemed like an eternity we were cleared for takeoff. One aircraft in my flight had a problem on the engine run up and had to abort the launch. Horse's flight had a similar problem after us but we finally got four planes in the air. The standard departure route turned north over the bay but that would have taken us right into the cloud. I turned my flight south to loop around the volcanic cloud to the east. Horse took his flight straight west over the water and then turned north.

As we climbed out I was able to get some pictures of the cloud. We were at 25,000 feet flying five miles to the east of Clark Air Base and the top of the cloud was well above us at over 45,000 feet. The irony of it was that the prevailing winds were out of the east. The entire cloud blew west and Clark sat in the sunshine while the cloud began to dump ash over Subic Bay where the Air Force had evacuated its people.

The flight to Kadena was uneventful and the squadron was able to get two more airplanes out the next day between eruptions before the field was closed. There were three eruptions that first day, and the easterly winds blew all the smoke and ash out over the South China Sea. A light dusting of ash landed on San Miguel, the Navy housing area on the coast at the west end of Lima Valley north of the bay. Clark was clear to the sun.

There were more eruptions on Thursday, and up to an inch of ash fell on Subic making the roads very slippery. One Filipino sailor was killed when he lost control of his car on the road to San Miguel and was broadsided by a bus. An old woman in San Marcelino on the coast was killed when she was hit by a rock hurled from the volcano nearly twenty miles away. The eruptions were getting stronger as the cloud tops were reported at above 66,000 feet. Still, we were laughing at the Air Force's folly.

The eruptions continued and by noon on Friday Subic Bay lost all power and water. In Okinawa we didn't know this until

Sunday, but the reality started to set in when all the phone lines went dead and CNN kept reporting that it was getting worse.

Saturday, June 15, Subic Bay became a living hell to many people. Over one hundred earthquakes shook the ground during the day and at 11:30 in the morning the big one that everyone had been predicting happened. Pinatubo blew its top 90,000 feet into the air. The winds in the upper atmosphere would eventually blow the cloud around the entire planet along the equator. To further compound matters, Typhoon Yunyi struck the Philippines with a fury. It hit the east coast near Manila, turned northwest and passed just east of Clark. The torrent of rain and high swirling winds turned the falling ash into a blizzard of hot mud that covered not only Subic Bay, but Clark as well, and spread as far as Manila, sixty-five miles away. At noon on Saturday it was darker than midnight at Subic Bay.

The rain mixed with the ash and fell with the consistency of cement weighing heavy on the roofs of buildings. Nipa huts and weaker structures were flattened and destroyed but larger buildings couldn't take the pressure either. Over fifty buildings on the naval base collapsed. In Olongapo and the surrounding towns hundreds of roofs fell in.

Lhey's home was in a small housing development called Roosevelt across the zigzag about five miles east of Olongapo. Her mother, Norma, woke her up at 10 a.m. She was worried. It was pitch black out and sand and rocks were falling like rain on the roof of their little three-room house. And then they began to feel the earthquakes. Lhey's twelve-year old cousin, Rowena, who was staying with them asked, "Are we going to die?"

Their water supply was already contaminated and shut off, but electric lines were still standing in the morning. Norma turned on the radio and heard an announcement warning people to clean off the roofs of their homes. Their house was on a slope, and not having a ladder, they put a 2x12 board on the slope above the house and set it down on the roof and then carefully crawled across and with a broom began sweeping the mud off. It was a good thing they did as one of the rafters in the house actually cracked, but they saved the roof. Two nearby neighbors had their roofs fall in and fled to Lhey's house for shelter.

A river where all the residents in the area did their laundry ran down a little valley about a hundred yards from the house. It was now just a mudflow and completely unusable. Fortunately I had taken seventeen gallons of water in Gatorade bottles out to the house about a week before we flew out. It wasn't enough for washing, but at least they had a small supply of drinking water.

Sixty miles away in Quezon City missionary Brenda Garren went to sleep on Friday night with her window open to catch the cool evening breeze. She woke up in the morning under a layer of dust two inches thick that had invaded her apartment. Farther away in Rojas, Palawan, two hundred miles to the southwest, missionary Harry Rogers and his family went to sleep Saturday night with the rhythm of a light rain, the fringe of the typhoon. They were woken up late in the night by the loud exhaust of a motor tricycle coming up the muddy road to their mission hospital. Owen Tan, a young man who worked with them, knocked at the door saying, "Mr. Rogers, it's raining milk." The light colored ash fall mixed with the rain had turned the water running down rain gutters and across the roads a milky white color.

At the height of the storm a U.S. destroyer in the South China Sea was ordered into Subic Bay. Facing the dark cloud the captain ordered all vents sealed with duct tape and the ship found its way into the bay in the middle of the storm by sonar. It would be the only source of fresh water for several days. Our exercise with the USS Abraham Lincoln was scrubbed and the Lincoln was diverted to Subic Bay to help with evacuation of non-essential personnel.

Thirty-six hours passed before the clouds began to clear and the first patch of blue sky appeared. In Barretto, a neighboring town on the north side of the bay, Chief Warrant Officer Richard Murphy lived with his Filipina girlfriend, Maritess. From his house he could actually see the flames thrusting upward from the volcano during the eruption. Great streaks of red lightning cracked horizontally across the darkness for hours. There was so much static in the air that the lightning flashes made the hair on his arms stand up. It shook him so much that he told God, "If you get us out of this I'll make an honest woman out of her."

And he did. He asked me to be in a sword arch as they left the church and placed me in the last position. "You know what to do?" he asked me. "Yes I do," I replied.

"Make sure you do it good," he said. When the ceremony was complete they left the church through the arch and when they passed me I swung my sword and whacked her with the flat side on the fanny so hard she jumped. "Welcome to the Navy," I said. "Murph" smiled his approval.

The devastation was horrific. Olongapo and surrounding towns looked like the bombed out cities in Germany in World War 2. The cement textured ash fall destroyed the paint and suspension of cars and collapsed buildings. Two to three feet of dust sat on the Subic Bay Naval Station and Olongapo as well as the entire area.

It was worse closer to the volcano. Prehistoric Valley no longer existed. The ravines were filled with mud and the foliage buried. Everywhere within a ten-mile radius of the volcano looked like the moon. As bad as it was only six hundred people were reported killed. Many of those were indigenous tribal people who lived around Pinatubo and worshipped the god of the mountain, *Apo Na*, refusing to leave when ordered to evacuate.

Mt. Pinatubo pumped more than five times as much ash into the air as Mt. St. Helens. In the months that followed the rains came and began washing the mud out of the mountain valleys. Crow Valley, our bombing range, was under four hundred feet of dirt and ash. When the rains began washing it out the mudflows, called *lahar,* washed everything in their paths away, including a corner of Clark Air Base.

The mudflows swept down the flood plains east of the mountains and buried entire towns up to the roofs of the houses and changed the shape of the landscape. The National Highway, which was our only route to Manila, was covered by so much mud that it was eventually elevated fifteen feet in places. When it rained the road was impassible.

The Air Force abandoned Clark recommending the Navy do the same, but the Navy had something the Air Force didn't have; Seabees. The Seabees went to work and in two weeks had the runway at Cubi Point cleared and opened for emergency supplies to be flown in. Not long after it was open for limited operations. Takeoffs and landings were separated by thirty-minute intervals to allow for the dust the jet wash stirred up to settle. Incoming aircraft had to time their arrivals to be landing within a ten-minute window. Departing aircraft had to be towed to the runway, washed off, and then started.

Because our emergency detachment had been unscheduled there was no room for us to stay at Kadena Air Base in Okinawa. We became a vagabond squadron, living in hotels in town for a while, and then relocating to Atsugi and eventually to Misawa, in northern Japan. Slowly we re-established communications with the squadron but it was July 6 before I was able to get word that Lhey and her family were all right. She had come down with a lung infection from the dust and had gone to Manila to stay with her cousin.

I was keeping a journal at the time and on July 8, I wrote the following about Lhey:

> If what I feel for her now is not the real thing, then there is no real thing. I've never been so lonesome in my life. Yesterday we had a sports day here. We played softball, football, and then basketball till we dropped. Then we played hoops again tonight. My feet hurt from it. When we got back though I was bored. I was bored all day. You know I would rather sit and do nothing as long as Lhey was there than to do everything when she's not.

Dennis and Shelia Potts were missionary friends of ours with Gospel Fellowship Missions in Manila. We had just visited them a couple weeks before the eruption and Dennis expressed his desire to perform our wedding. We decided that as soon as all the paperwork was done we would elope to Manila and then plan a ceremony at the church the next November. All that was left was for Lhey to get her physical at St. Luke's hospital in Manila. Then the volcano erupted.

Six weeks passed before I was able to lead a flight back down to the Philippines. It was strange flying over what looked like a wasteland as we came in. The smell of sulfur was heavy in the air even invading our cockpits at 10,000 feet. What was most discouraging, however, was that the local Civil Registrar's Office, which had some of the documents we needed had been destroyed. The paperwork was lost, and we essentially had to start over getting Lhey's documents together.

The reason for our planned elopement was that the United States and the Philippines were negotiating for the renewal of the lease on the American military bases. An anti-American contingent in the government wanted us out and the negotiations did not seem to be going well. The Philippine position was that if the agreement was not renewed we had to leave the country by September 16, the day the lease ran out. The U.S. position was that we had one year by the current treaty to evacuate. Not knowing what was going to happen we wanted to get Lhey's name on my documents as soon as possible so if we had to leave she could go with me.

We went back to work and in a few weeks had recovered all the documents. I went to the Navy marriage office near the Philippine military liaison office on the base to turn in all the paperwork. A Filipino secretary told me we needed one more thing. I went and got Lhey and we procured the missing document. The next time I brought it in another secretary said I needed something else. So we went and got it.

The third time I tried to submit our materials the secretary passed me on to a Lt.j.g. who was in charge of the office. She looked it over and said to me, "Well you really don't have everything you need."

At that point I almost exploded. I told her I wasn't trying to sneak anything by, that I was trying to get everything I need, but every time I went in there I was told I needed something else. "Just tell me everything I need so we can get this done," I said. She looked at my paperwork again and said, "Well I guess this will do." Duh!

All we could do then was wait. I called Dennis Potts and they were on standby. The only other people who knew the plan were Lhey's mother, Norma, and her Aunt Wilma, and our pastor, Henry Senina and his wife, Nenita. On September 8, I finally got the notification that we were approved. The next morning I checked out on leave, picked up Lhey and Norma, called Dennis to tell him we were on the way and went to the bus station. That was the easy part.

The rains had closed the old highway and our bus tried an alternate route through the town of Guagua. The highway itself was under two feet of water at the junction, but the town was flooded and we couldn't get through. So after waiting an hour for the waters to recede our driver decided to try the old highway. It was covered with mud and no vehicle had crossed it in a week. At the highway our driver and conductor got out and walked on the road to see how solid it was and decided to try it. The driver got up a head of steam and we raced across the section that had been closed. It was about two and a half miles long but we made it across. The trip to Manila was normally about two and a half to three hours, but this trip took five.

We reached the Potts' home in Quezon City around four. They had gathered witnesses including Brenda Garren and we had our ceremony, and went out to Pizza Hut for our wedding dinner with everyone. Then we went to the airport for our honeymoon trip to Hong Kong. (No, Norma didn't go with us.)

The journey home was worse than the trip to Manila. Our bus tried Guagua again but it was still under two feet of water and after waiting nearly two hours the driver decided when the water started coming in the door of the bus to try the highway. Just about sunset we came to a spot that had been washed out. Another bus was stuck in the middle of it. Occasionally a four-wheel drive vehicle would plow through the dip but the bus couldn't make it. We were the third bus from the washout but the line of buses and other vehicles behind us was growing.

We waited another two hours and I decided to step out with some other men for some fresh air. I carefully set my left foot down on gravel that was solid, but when I put my right foot down not ten inches away it sunk down to my ankle in the mud.

At last a front-end loader came, pushed the bus out of the ditch and then shoveled the mud to level the road. When he was done he simply drove away, but the bus drivers were still afraid to try. We waited some more until finally one attempted it, got across, and then our driver gunned it and followed. It took us seven hours to get home.

When we returned from Hong Kong we informed the rest of the family and then planned a formal wedding ceremony at our church (First Olongapo Fundamental Baptist) in December. At first we had wanted to just keep it a secret until the church wedding because eloping in the Philippines carries a bad connotation with it, but we were afraid with time the secret was going to leak out so we decided to tell the church. When Pastor

Senina announced it one Sunday morning all the members cheered and told us they approved of what we had done.

Olongapo was a notorious Navy port call. For many of the sailors stationed at Subic Bay it was a "Good Time Charlie" tour. The city's economy was basically built around bars and prostitution. It was a morass of sin and destroyed the morals and lives of a lot of young sailors and Marines. I had come across a gospel tract in Tagalog that had a clear salvation message. After work at the squadron I used the Xerox machine to make three thousand copies while waiting for an order of the tract to come from the publisher. Some of the people from the church helped me pass them out all over town. About the same time some Pentecostal groups had taken to street preaching warning people that God's judgment was coming.

Some of the pilots asked me one day what I thought about God's judgment and if that's what Mt. Pinatubo was. I said it could be. God's mercy is great but the Bible says He will not always strive with men. They got defensive and Horse asked, "Why? What have these poor people ever done to anybody?"

"Are you crazy?" I said. The whole town is a prostitution ring. You guys go out there and indulge yourselves all the time. It's an abomination to God, a violation of the Seventh Commandment, and He warns us over and over in the Bible against it. All these young sailors ruining their lives, getting diseases. What do you think?" They had no answer.

Lhey and I lived in my BOQ (Bachelor Officer Quarters) room for three months, which technically was not allowed, until a house became available for us in Bayani Village, a housing area on a slope on the east side of the base near the golf course. Every time we drove by the links we would see Negritoes walking along the road. Negrito is a generic term used to describe the aboriginal people in the South Pacific islands because of their dark skin and curly hair. There are many different tribal groups in the Philippines but the people in our region were known as the *Aeta* (Eye-tuh).

Chapter Two
A Little Village in the Jungle

In the aftermath of the eruption there were a hundred thousand refugees in camps around Olongapo. The largest was below a forty-foot tall statue of Mary along the highway from Subic town on the north side of the bay going north to the town of Castilillejos. Tens of thousands of people lived in makeshift tents and depended on daily deliveries of water from the government. A nursing station was set up to help with medical emergencies, but the people had little possessions or food.

I had the only car in our church and one Sunday I went to the pastor and offered to drive people out to the refugee center on Saturdays if he wanted to start a ministry there. I wrote to my home church, South Sheridan Baptist in Denver, Colorado, and the people responded sending twelve boxes of clothes. We also received donations from the church people and other churches around Luzon began sending canned goods and other food items.

We divided the food and clothes into plastic bags and every Saturday morning we just about shoehorned nine or ten people into my little Chevette and made the trip to the statue. We started going through the camp talking with people and sharing the gospel. To those who would listen we would invite them down to the car when we were done and give them a bag of goods.

There was one particular group of people that had come from across the river in a small town called Omaya. With the river full of mud and flooding from the rains they couldn't get back across for six months. Their leader was a little man, Carlos, who was shorter than Lhey, who is five foot two. He was the first to accept the Lord and when transportation became available he began bringing his family and neighbors down to our church services on Sundays. Eventually about two hundred people trusted the Lord and when they were able to return to their homes we helped them build a church building.

The refugee camp also presented me with my greatest challenge in speaking Tagalog. I had never taken a formal class but had picked up the language at church and with Lhey and her family. I was conversational at best and while most of the people in Olongapo spoke English to some degree, many of the refugees were not so well versed. I memorized John 3:16 in Tagalog and was able to share it often. I never led anyone to the Lord using Tagalog, but the experience helped me along with the language.

One day at the refugee camp I was with Pastor Al Bondad. We were talking with a group when one half drunk man suddenly fell to his knees in front of me, grabbed my hand and started kissing it, and cried, "*Banal*" (Holy). I quickly withdrew my hand and said, "No, get up! I'm just a man like you are." It actually scared me to think someone might be trying to worship me like some kind of holy man. I thought of Paul and Barnabas at Lystra in Acts 14 when the people wanted to offer sacrifices to them thinking they were gods. I looked at Al and said, "I wonder if this was how Paul and Barnabas felt." He just laughed.

Our church had sent Al Bondad to start a new work in the Roosevelt area near where Lhey's house was located. I helped with the purchase of the land and as a building started going up Pastor Al invited me to come and speak. I was reluctant at first. I was a pilot, not a preacher, but because I had graduated from Bob Jones University, a fundamental Bible school, everybody thought I should know how. Henry Senina had assigned me to preach without even asking several times at the church. So I agreed and went to help Al. I'm not sure if I was a real help or not, but I did gain some experience at preaching as a layman. Al and I became good friends and he was a groomsman in our wedding.

On the base I kept seeing the *Aeta* people along the road and by early 1992 the Lord began to lay a real burden on my heart for them. We knew they lived somewhere near a bend in the road behind a jungle covered hill. I talked with Lhey about meeting them sometime and she agreed. Then I talked with Pastor Al also and he was excited to go with me.

We decided on a Saturday and I picked him up and we drove to the curve. There was a shoulder wide enough to pull over and park on so we stopped and got out. There was a small trail that went around the hill and the village was not far behind it. There were only ten or twelve families living there in what could have been considered to be more of a campground than a village. The homes were no more than hootches, large sections of canvass or plastic draped over tree branches. A few had some boards nailed between trees for walls and a couple of places had corrugated tin roofs over their canvass or bamboo slat walls.

Their furniture consisted of 2x12 boards for beds or benches, a few camp chairs and small fold up or makeshift wood tables.

There were only about fifty people in all and as we came around the hill into the village they seemed happy to see us. It may have been just curiosity but as we mingled they were very open and talked, all in Tagalog. Most of this group spoke little or no English. Two men stood out, however. One was named Fletcher Abraham, the other Domingo. Fletcher was barely five feet tall and kept his head shaved. He said that he was the chairman of the village. The village was called Pamulaklakin. Fletcher seemed proud and aloof and didn't talk to us very much.

The entire area around the golf course all the way to Boton, where a Marine detachment was staged close to the Cubi runway, and up into the mountains behind the village was the ancestral homeland of this *Aeta* tribe. There was another small group camped out on the opposite side of the fairway and others lived farther up in the mountains.

At Boton was a JEST (Jungle Environmental Survival Training) camp. Some of the *Aeta* men worked as instructors there. Others acted as guides for the U.S. Marines who daily patrolled the perimeter of the naval station guarding against communist NPA (New People's Army) guerilla incursions. The NPA controlled large portions of the Bataan peninsula right up to the boundaries of the base and were a bigger problem than most Americans probably realized. Subic Bay was the largest American naval station in the world outside the United States and the perimeter ran for twenty-two miles through the jungle.

The NPA's fight was with the Marcos regime, but when Marcos was overthrown in 1986 and Cory Aquino extended an olive branch to them they had no cause. The removal of the U.S. bases then became their *reason d'etre* and in October 1987, a "Sparrow unit," an NPA hit squad, murdered two American Airmen outside the gate at Clark three days before I transferred back to the States. I wound up being on the plane with one of the families and when our flight stopped in Guam I spoke with them for a few minutes and offered my condolences.

The NPA problem had worsened by the time I returned to the Philippines in January 1990. Two more Americans were killed in Angeles and we were put on a very restricted liberty area and had to be off the streets by 11 p.m. One Sunday night a Marine

Gunny Sergeant was killed two blocks away from our church. I had just passed the corner on my way back to the base twenty minutes before the attack took place. It was first thought that it was another Sparrow unit action, but it turned out that the Gunny had a reputation for being rude to Filipinos and on this particular night he had abused and offended someone to the point of revenge by murder. I have found that Filipinos are easily offended and they don't take offenses lightly.

Olongapo City is much smaller and compact geographically than Angeles where Clark Air Base was located, and easier for Military Police to patrol, but we were still warned to take extra care about our personal security when in town. Traveling out of town we were required to stay on the National Highway to either Angeles or Manila. All travel on the Bataan Peninsula was prohibited.

Bataan was south of the base and a great place to fly. There was no other aviation around and I loved to fly low around the dormant Mariveles volcano and over Corregidor Island. It was also a convenient area to do functional check flights (FCF) on the A-4 when Cubi was landing on runway 25 to the southwest. The A-4 had a regular maintenance schedule, which included periodic complete tear down inspections. These and any maintenance involving a control surface required a check flight before the plane could be rescheduled for operational flights. As it turned out I was the only FCF check pilot in the squadron at the time, so I got them all.

FCFs were actually a lot of fun until the last check. From takeoff at Cubi I would turn south toward Lubang Island climbing to 37,000 feet checking the instrument readings at designated altitudes. From there I rolled it over and dived nose straight down. If I had no external fuel tanks I'd let it accelerate as fast as I could get it. The A-4 was stressed to 1.3 Mach, but the engine couldn't get it there in level flight. In the dive, however, I could push it to about 1.1 mach. Going through transonic speed at about .99 to 1.0 Mach the controls turned to mush and I was essentially a rock hurdling toward earth. At 25,000 feet I'd throttle back and immediately the plane slowed out of Mach speed and then I'd pull the nose up hard to check the G-suit system and level it off at 15,000 for the final checks.

One afternoon I had a lot of extra fuel and time to burn. A cloud hung over a volcano island next to Lubang called Ambil, and out of it a rainbow extended to the side and arced down to the ocean. I wondered what it would be like to fly through a rainbow so I pointed my nose at the bow and flew toward it. What looked small at first grew wider as I came in on it, but then, like an optical illusion, it seemed to hold its position in front of me and I couldn't close with it. Then all at once I was engulfed in the colors that faded quickly away as rain spattered my windscreen. I jokingly wondered if I was in Oz, then flew around to see if the rainbow was still there and did it again.

All of the rides weren't that easy or relaxed. One afternoon I took a plane up for an FCF, did all the regular checks, and at 15,000 feet over Bataan prepared for the last item. The A-4 had only one hydraulic system and if it failed the plane had to be flown manually which required the system to be disconnected. The ailerons had to be trimmed so that when the plane was disconnected it would remain in level flight. A role rate of five degrees per second with hands off the controls was the maximum allowed.

I trimmed the plane level at 250 knots, took my hands off the stick and prepared to disconnect. The disconnect handle was on the right side at the bottom of the instrument panel. I had my left hand next to the stick and with my right hand reached down and pulled the handle. The plane rolled violently left so fast that the stick slapped my hand and I was nearly inverted with the nose pointing sixty degrees down before I could get my right hand on the stick and stop the roll. Even with both hands on the stick I was unable to roll it back over. I thought for an instant of letting it roll on around to complete an aileron roll but I wasn't sure if I let it continue I'd be able to stop the role or pull the nose up. The next brief moment I thought of giving the plane back to the taxpayers and ejecting, but I was over NPA controlled territory, and in another moment I was accelerating through 400 knots which was the maximum safe ejection airspeed.

With my left hand I quickly reached for the throttle and pulled it back to idle, put it back on the stick and then with my right thumb used the electric trim tab on the stick to reposition the left aileron to try to stop the roll. By then I was passing through 10,000 feet, the recommended out of control ejection altitude, but the trim tab worked and by 7,000 I had regained control, rolled the plane up and pulled it out of the dive at 5,000 feet.

As near as I could figure the plane had rolled at more than 120 degrees per second. The entire incident had taken no more than thirty seconds, and if I hadn't regained control I had even less time than that to live. Wasn't there an old saying that went, "The Lord takes care of fools and pilots?" I'm not sure which one I was but the Lord took care of me that day.

The NPA had threatened to kill more Americans and the last place I wanted to be was out in the jungle somewhere in Bataan. The jungle I did look forward to visiting was by the golf course. The *Aeta* people had no political agenda. They lived primitively but greatly appreciated the security that came from living on the American military base. They were proud to be able to work for the Americans and were more than happy to have us come and visit with them.

Over the next few visits Pastor Al began to share the gospel and eight adults, four women and four men, prayed to accept the Lord. But Fletcher resisted. "No," he said. "I don't need that." "Why not?" we asked. "Because I have never sinned," he replied. At that comment Domingo burst out laughing and put his arm around Fletcher's shoulders. "Oh, you've sinned," he shouted. "I know you have."

A few days later I brought Lhey down to the village. We parked the car along the road and walked around the hill back into the trees. The adults were excited to see her and talked more openly with her than with Al or myself. There were a number of children running around and Lhey asked the women if we could come and have a Bible story time with the children. They readily agreed. "We'll be here on Sunday morning," we told them.

On Sunday morning before we went out to church we stopped by the hill and made our way into the village. The women gathered the children and ushered them to a 2x12 board nailed up between two trees for a bench. The children sat attentively as Lhey began to tell them stories from the Bible illustrating God's love for them. They began to expect us each Sunday morning. We didn't have to gather them up because they would already be on the bench waiting for us when we arrived. Over the next few weeks twelve of the children prayed with Lhey and asked Jesus into their hearts.

It was June 1992 and had the Navy base stayed open we would have continued our visits with the *Aetas* until the next January when I would have had orders out. But the times were strange and there was a strong anti-American faction in the government. None other than the president, Cory Aquino, had encouraged them.

After the People's Power revolution that overthrew Ferdinand Marcos, she was established as the new president over a government that was anything but stable. She would eventually survive four coup attempts herself. One of the criticisms against her was that she was a puppet of Ronald Reagan and the American government. In order to distance herself from that accusation she began to lobby against a renewal of the bases agreement. The Filipino negotiator, Raul Manglapus, played hardball with the U.S. negotiator, Richard Armitage, demanding much more than the U.S. was willing to give.

An agreement was finally reached and Aquino, perhaps suddenly realizing she would be losing American support against the NPA as well as hundreds of millions in aid annually, started lobbying in favor of the agreement. It seems to have been too little too late. The Philippine Senate required a two-thirds majority vote to pass any treaty with a foreign power. With twenty-four senators they only needed sixteen yes votes, but came up one short.

The U.S. Navy would have to leave, but we were given one year to depart. We were in the process of drawing down and flying our last few missions before decommissioning our squadron, VC-5, permanently. In fact, our A-4s were so old that we began flying them off to a maintenance facility at Atsugi, Japan where they were to be retired and mothballed. When I took Checkertail (our call sign) 03 up to Japan, I flew the last A-4 still flying that had received battle damage in Vietnam.

I had orders back to the States the first week of June and as we came to our last Sunday in the country we made one last stop at the village to see the children. Lhey taught their Bible story and when she was done she talked with some of the ladies. One woman who was there visiting said to Lhey, "I wish you could come to our village. We have many more children than this." We asked about her village and as near as I could figure from her description it was about three kilometers up in the mountains. Our hearts were broken because we were leaving the country the next day.

I went around and shook hands with the men including Fletcher, and determined at that moment to begin praying for Fletcher and Domingo. We said goodbye and started for the car and all the children followed after us. They climbed up on the ridge to wave and Lhey went up to give everyone of them a hug.

At the car we waved again and as we climbed in tears rolled down Lhey's face. When hugging the children one little girl told her, "When you leave I will cry." We both had tears as we drove away slowly, hardly wanting to lose sight of the kids on the hill, and wondering if we would ever be able to see them again.

Chapter Three
The Road to the Mission Field

My uncle, Dr. Carl Boonstra, along with his life long friend, Rev. Clifford Clark, were two of the chief promoters of a method of supporting missions in churches called Faith Promise, a concept first conceived by Oswald J. Smith, a Presbyterian minister in Toronto, Canada. After sixteen years as a pastor in Denver, Colorado, Dr. Boonstra spent his next sixteen years as the Mission Director of the Baptist Bible Fellowship, Int. in Springfield Missouri, a fellowship of over 4500 independent Baptist churches.

It is not surprising then that his church, East Side Baptist, was a very mission minded church. Every year we had a mission conference in tandem with another Baptist church in town and would bring in eight or ten missionaries and swap them back and forth between the two churches for a week of meetings on missions. They presented scores of foreign fields to us. We were the sending church for two families, the Stricklands in Argentina, and the Konnerups in Ethiopia. Both of these families had been friends of my parents since the their high school days. All of our families had children in the same age range, and we all became lifelong friends as well. Missions was in my blood.

When I was fourteen and my Sunday school teachers, Curt and Louise Hokanson, proposed a mission trip for the teens there was no way I was going to miss it. The preparation became somewhat of a contest to make sure those going were serious about the purpose, and not just taking a vacation. We had to memorize fifty Bible verses, invite friends to Sunday school, and have nearly perfect church attendance over a six-month period to qualify to go.

There were ten of us, two guys and eight girls, that eventually made the trip to the Navajo Indian reservation at Crownpoint, New Mexico, where we helped missionaries Harry and Maxine Philips and their daughter Mary with a week long Vacation Bible School. It was a great experience and a defining moment in my youth. Missions had become a part of my life. I prayed for the Philips for as long as they lived and Mary has remained a life-long friend. One winter years later as I was traveling across New Mexico, a blizzard closed I-40 at the exit to

Crownpoint. So I turned off and drove on up to the Philips' place unannounced and they put me up for the night. Later when Lhey and I became missionaries their Navajo church supported our ministry.

I went to college on the long plan, worked my way through, and took my time trying to figure out what I really wanted to do. For a while I chased a baseball dream, which was a dead end. Then I took the Missions course at Baptist Bible College in Springfield Missouri for two years but I didn't feel a particular call to the mission field. For one I had been painfully shy as a child and although I had a burden for missions I couldn't see myself as a preacher and felt no specific leading to that work.

Eventually I graduated with a degree in history from Bob Jones University, went to Officer Candidate School in Quantico, Virginia and became a Marine officer. From there it was off to flight school in Pensacola, Florida and Beeville, Texas, and in November 1984 I earned my wings as a Marine aviator. Then came another one of those defining moments in my life.

I had first applied to the Navy but was turned down for officer programs because my degree was from Bob Jones. BJU is a bastion of biblical fundamentalism and an early leader in the theological battle against modernism, which denies the Virgin Birth and blood atonement of Christ. BJU stands solidly for the inspiration of the Scriptures and a literal interpretation of them.

They also held a very strict conviction in a certain controversial area concerning race and interracial dating relationships on campus. The policy was changed in 2000, but in 1981 it didn't sit well with someone in the Department of the Navy. As a result somebody in the Navy had set a policy against BJU that was actually a violation of the Navy's own recruiting regulations. My pastor at the time, Dr. Ed Nelson, helped me with an appeal to Colorado Senator Bill Armstrong and South Carolina Senator Strom Thurmond, who was a member of the Board of Trustees at BJU, but the appeals failed. So I took my application to the Marine Corps and was accepted.

Now almost four years later the Marine Corps had over recruited pilots, and with the Reagan military build up the Navy was in need of carrier pilots. I was at MCAS Yuma, Arizona on April 1, 1985 when they called two hundred Marine pilots into a semi-circular tiered lecture hall and told us our future as pilots was with the Navy. Of all the people there I had the temerity to ask a question. "It's April first. Are you sure we can trust you?"

After the laughter died down they assured us it wasn't a joke. We all were already scheduled to meet a Navy detailer to discuss orders. Leaving the Marine Corps wasn't mandatory, but they painted a bleak picture for our future if we didn't go. I walked into the meeting and told the Navy Commander I wasn't interested. I was flying A-4Ms and I wasn't interested in going to sea.

"Well wait a minute," he said. "I can give you A-4s and shore based orders." I said where, and he said, "The Philippines."

The thought that struck me in the heart at that moment was "mission field," and I immediately knew that was what God wanted. I had five days to decide and I spent the entire time arguing with the Lord against going to the Navy. I loved the Marine Corps and didn't want to change, but in the end the burden on my heart was to go. I made the switch, spent two years in the Philippines, then went back to the training command as an instructor for two more years, and when I was offered a job as an instructor in the flight program at Bob Jones I determined to resign and leave the Navy.

I put in my letter to resign but while checking out I had to visit the commanding officer at the base, Captain Bertch. He took a liking to me and asked if there were any orders I would take to stay in the Navy. I said I would go back to VC-5, my old squadron in the Philippines. He told me he had a friend at the Pentagon who owed him a favor and asked me if I would reconsider if he could get the orders for me.

I said I would, thinking it would never happen, but two weeks later I had the orders in hand and I withdrew my resignation. So essentially what happened was this. The Navy turned me down for reasons that amounted to nothing short of a policy of religious persecution, then wanted me to fill a need for carrier pilots, but at my demand gave me shore based orders to the Philippines, not once, but twice to the same place, something that almost never happens in the military, and something that didn't meet their need for carrier pilots, and I got on the job training in mission work at the Navy's expense. God got even with the Navy for their policy.

And then the Navy did more. I had taken the mandatory freshman speech at BJU and a pulpit speech class at BBC, but I didn't do well in either. I studied music for two years and took voice lessons, but speaking to large audiences just wasn't my cup of tea.

It was the Marine Corps that toughened me up and brought me out of my shell and the Navy gave me the opportunity to prove it. At VC-5 I had jobs in several shops as a Branch Officer, but then became the Training Officer and on my second tour the Safety Officer. We had training and safety stand-downs twice a year. Listening to people give boring technical lectures that put everyone to sleep I kept thinking I could do better than this, and finally I had my chance.

As the Training Officer I planned an entire day of lectures and demonstrations and wound up giving the final speech myself. I spiced it up with illustrations and jokes, employing things that I had learned in the speech classes and had the place in stitches before I was done. Speaking to over 350 people I had overcome any remnant of shyness and found that I enjoyed speaking to the crowds.

The crowning moment came when I gave my last safety lecture at VC-5 before introducing the base chaplain to be our final speaker. There had been an ALLNAV (All Navy) message that had been sent on the subject of drunk driving. It was a subject I had been passionate about because a Navy friend of mine and two of his three children had been killed by a drunk driver, and his wife and third child injured so badly they couldn't even attend the funeral. I turned to I Corinthians 6:9-10 and paraphrased slightly to say, "no drunk drivers," will be in heaven. Then when I introduced the chaplain he came up and put his cross collar emblem on my collar and made me an honorary chaplain. The entire squadron cheered.

Perhaps the hardest day of my life came in July 1989 when we had an aircraft go down. I was the acting Safety Officer for VT-25 at NAS Chase Field in Beeville, Texas while we waited for another pilot who was at Safety School in Monterrey, California to arrive. Life goes through ups and downs and there are times when you are in the downs and everything seems to go wrong that you can almost think you are jinxed. It started on a Monday when one of our students in a TA-4 doing practice landings for carrier qualifications at NAS Goliad flew into the ground in a turn.

The next day I was the Squadron Duty Officer and as I sat at the Ready Room desk by the big tinted window looking out over our flight line just at dusk a T-2 training aircraft from NAS Kingsville crashed on takeoff killing the pilot and injuring the student. Two days later we had one of our TA-4s with a brake failure on landing run off the end of the runway. No one was injured in that incident, but the Commanding Officer cancelled all flights for Friday and told me to put together an emergency safety stand down.

After our TA-4 crashed I was out in a field north of Goliad with the emergency crew looking through the wreckage trying to figure out what had happened. The plane had hit the ground at about 400 knots airspeed, caught a big mesquite tree at the wing root and tumbled for about 400 yards breaking into a million pieces. You can imagine what it did to the pilot's body.

I had flown with this student a few times, most recently just two weeks before. It had been my practice to give a gospel tract to each new student I flew with and invite them to church, but as I was putting body parts into plastic bags all I could think was had I done enough? I gave the last lecture at the stand down on Friday and challenged the squadron to consider their own lives, would they be ready if they faced the same dilemma?

I told Lhey before we got married that I had a burden for missions and we might be missionaries someday, but after I got out of the Navy and we had our first son the thought of actually becoming a missionary had drifted to the back of my mind. But Lhey also had a burden for missions and when she had been in Bible college in the Philippines she saw a picture in an article of a primitive African man and said, "Lord, if you call me to the mission field, please send me to Africa."

After eleven years I was tired of military life and got out of the Navy. I taught at Silver State Baptist School in Denver for two years and then got back into flying as a co-pilot on a Westwind 1 owned by Denver Bronco quarterback John Elway. The fun part of the job was meeting the owner, but the crew concept in flying was boring and now that I had a family I lost interest in being gone on long trips all the time. Then it became complicated.

Our church held a weeklong mission conference and since we had no trips on the plane that week Lhey and I went to all the meetings. On the second night the Lord was speaking to me heavily about surrendering to go to the mission field. By that time I was already forty-two and I kept thinking I'm too old to make this change now. But the burden continued and as we stood during the invitation at the end of the message I finally prayed, "Lord, if you're going to call me you have to call Lhey too."

I no sooner prayed that thought in my heart than Lhey put her hand in mine and said, "Let's go forward." He was speaking to her and I could no longer resist. We went and prayed and surrendered to go to the mission field.

But now I had a problem. Elway had a partner in the plane and when I was hired the president of the partner's company, who actually wrote the checks, asked me to commit to staying with them for two years. I had about twenty-one months to go. I was already unhappy with the job, drilling straight lines through the sky on autopilot was mundane, but determined to keep my word until about eight months later when the Lord worked it out for me to leave.

Since I had gotten out of the Navy three missionary families that were friends of mine in Kenya had been encouraging us to pray about working with them. Richard Konnerup was the first to broach the subject with us. His first wife, Jeannine, had been my mother's best friend in high school. Then his son, Ole, who had been my best friend in high school, spoke to me about it. Then Jerry Daniels, who had been my Sunday school teacher at one time, encouraged us about Kenya. We had prayed about it for a long time, but now that it looked like the door was open the Philippines seemed like the more logical place to go. I was uncertain, and Lhey didn't seem to be real excited about Africa.

One evening we had missionaries Jimmy and Marie Strickland, who were home on furlough from Argentina, over for dinner. As we talked I mentioned Richard Konnerup encouraging us to go to Kenya, but I had a house full of rosewood furniture that I had purchased in Hong Kong and had shipped on my orders home. What was I to do with all this stuff?

Jimmy tightened his lips into a slight smile, raised his eyebrows, as he was wont to do, took a deep breath and looked me straight in the eye. "It's easy to become comfortable," he said.

There was nothing condemning or critical in his comment, just an affectionate observation, and I've never forgotten it. It's easy to become comfortable.

Then one day in my devotions I read Isaiah 30:21, "Thine ears shall hear a voice behind thee saying, this is the way, walk ye in it, when ye turn to the right hand or when ye turn to the left." Lord, I prayed, what way do you want me to go? Everything I do seems to be the right or the left hand. The answer came into my head as clear as if someone had spoken it, "What have you been praying about?"

I knew then we had to go to Kenya. I told Lhey and she said okay. We immediately applied to be missionaries with the Baptist Bible Fellowship, Int. and started raising our support before we were even approved.

The one question we got everywhere we went on deputation was why not the Philippines? We could only say that this was where God had called us. After twenty-two months of deputation we departed for Kenya in February 1999.

Years before the Navy had a recruiting slogan that said, "The Navy: it's not a job, it's an adventure." We were about to find that living in Africa was just that, not a job, but an adventure.

Chapter Four
Africa

There is a mystique about Africa. It gets under your skin. It calls you. The vast expanse of the veldt with magnificent danger lurking behind every hill and tree; the grandeur of Kilimanjaro so massive not even Everest matches its appeal; untamable wildlife, loose, walking where you walk; the hair raising percussion of a lion's roar slapping your chest in the dark; the curiosity of a giraffe coming face to face with your car on the road and bending down to look in your windshield before galloping off; life in the bush that is so simple it defies the banality of civilized existence; people whose very survival depends on a daily trip to a muddy river for water to filter and drink, and which is so scarce they've rarely if ever bathed completely; body odors that are so acrid they almost burn your nose until you get used to them. Yet, you do get used to them, and once you have been there, you forever have a yearning to go back.

Living for fourteen years in Kenya was in many ways an adventure, yet in many others it was an existence that defied all that is rational. We lived a half mile across an open field from Kenyatta University and saw the futility of life yearly, almost as if it was a part of the scheduled curriculum.

While most Kenyans struggled to survive, many begging missionaries or other ex-pats to pay the way for their children in private schools so they could get some pretense of an education, the rich kids, of whom there was a small class, went off to universities to get a degree for who knew what purpose since with a 60% unemployment rate there was little hope for a job after graduation. Every year as the last school term came close to an end the students rioted, tearing up the grounds and destroying property on the campus. The highway outside the front gate would be blocked until the police came and a standoff would ensue until teargas was fired and the school would be closed for the remainder of the term. You could set your calendar by it. It was a miracle that anyone ever graduated.

The most common form of transportation in Kenya is the *matatu*, a Nissan minivan that serves as a bus. They are the most dangerous vehicles on the road as they race down the highways defying all traffic laws. One Saturday a *matatu* hit a young woman crossing the highway at Kenyatta University and killed her. The *matatu* raced on without stopping.

The university was between our house and the church in Kihunguro. The next morning crowds of students were gathering along the road when we went to church. On our way home the crowd milling about had grown but was still calm. As we passed by slowly several waved and smiled at us. Thirty minutes later the quiet mob went demonic and started attacking cars that dared go by. A small water truck was set ablaze along with several cars, but when the riot was quelled, not one of the destroyed vehicles was a *matatu*. There was no sense to any of it.

Matatus made up forty-five percent of the vehicles on the road. The drivers were arrogant, the *touts* (conductors) were vicious street brawlers, and they were involved in half of all accidents on the roads. To say they were dangerous was an understatement, but they were the way of life for most people that had to travel. I rode in one with twenty-six passengers crammed inside. Once was all I needed to experience.

The Kenya Automobile Association (AA, like America's AAA) published an article in 2001 that stated that seventy-five percent of all injury related traffic accidents in the world took place in sub-Saharan Africa where ten percent of the world's population lives. That should tell you everything you need to know.

Everybody has their stories about the worst drivers in the world being in Thailand, the Philippines, Italy, all over South America, and who knows where else, but I was glad when my cousin, Sharon, who had been a missionary in Ecuador for twenty-nine years came over for a visit and saw what we had to deal with. She couldn't believe how crazy the drivers were, or that Lhey drove in the traffic without batting an eye. I've often said I'd rather drive in Manila with its 18 million people and impossible jams than in Nairobi.

When the government tried to clamp down on the *matatus* and restrict the number of passengers in a vehicle to fourteen the drivers and touts went on strike. I was on my way to language school one morning when I ran into a riot at the first roundabout going south from our home. A car ahead of me had all of its windows smashed by stones. We had a four-wheel drive Land Rover Discovery and I turned off the road and went across a field to get away, but I still had one side window smashed and several dents in the fenders before I got away and made the trip back home with a large rock on the roof.

Our first year in Kenya was a rough one. I had skin rashes on my legs that burned and wouldn't quit, and dandruff so bad that my scalp actually bled and scabbed over. Lhey had constant bouts with anemia and was always tired, and our son Jonathan had food poisoning twice. We had no running water. Instead we had an 1800-gallon water tank in the ground from which we pumped water to a 250-gallon tank in the attic which gravity fed the house. The country was in a draught and twice our water level got so low we had to ration water until we could find a water truck to refill it.

On Easter Sunday 2000 our house with all its iron gates and locks was broken into while we were at church. Our night guard, Ezekiel, had gone with us to the service so that no one was at the house. Lhey had not been feeling well that morning and almost stayed home, but at the last minute she decided to go. It was a good thing she did.

When we came home we found the gate open. The thieves had managed to get a crow bar under the big iron doors on our garage and lift the bolt in the floor out of place, slide it open and walk right in. They took all our electronics; computer, laptop, stereo, VCRs, cameras and video camera, my collection of Cincinnati Pops CDs, and other non-electric things. They ransacked the house, although they weren't cruel and didn't smash windows or mirrors or destroy anything. Clothes and mattresses were strewn about and we were distraught.

I stood in the hallway upstairs thinking, "Why God? We come here to help these people and this is what we get for it?" At that moment I just felt like it was enough, I didn't want to put my family through this, and I wanted to go home. Then Jonathan came running up to me from his room. Just the day before he'd gotten a new batman toy.

"Dad, Dad!" he said excitedly. "Look. They didn't get my batman!" He held it out to show me. "And you don't have to worry about the cameras. You can use mine." He handed me his toy plastic camera.

I knelt down and hugged him, hardly able to hold back the tears. My five-year-old son had put it all in perspective. They were just things. We weren't hurt. Although it would take a while we would get over it. At least the thieves didn't get any money. We were in a building project and I had a lot of cash at the house, but I'd hidden it well and they didn't find it. Lhey had also hidden some money in the pant leg of a pair of jeans and even though our clothes were strewn all over they didn't find it either.

Three nights later our faith was shaken again when at two o'clock in the morning we heard eight shots fired from two guns. Thieves were trying to break into a neighbor's house three doors down from our own, but the neighbor also had a gun and drove them off. By the time we went home three years later there had been five shootings in our neighborhood, three of them with fatalities.

The police came to investigate but they were almost worthless. Ezekiel's brother was a police captain and he made calls to make sure a forensic team came to our house to get fingerprints. It didn't really do any good because there is no database to make comparisons with in Kenya, but they made the effort. I realized, however, that the investigation was going nowhere when the police detective started asking me who I wanted him to arrest. When he asked me one day to drive him to Nakuru two hours away to follow up a lead I said no and that was essentially the end of the investigation.

What really hurt us was that after we started trying to put things together all the circumstantial evidence pointed to people we knew, whom we had invited into our house for Christmas dinner. People we had shown kindnesses to. We lived on the corner of two dirt roads and the dust was endless. We had hired a maid, a church member in one of the churches we worked with, to help Lhey cleaning the house. When she came to work the day after the robbery Lhey told her to clean the kitchen, but she took a cloth and first began to wipe down the walls in the living room where the stolen items had been. Her cousins who had asked if they could plant crops on the yard between our fence and the road and were there almost daily never came back, and her husband suddenly had money to buy his own *matatu*.

We couldn't prove anything really, but others who worked for us, who saw what was happening and could have warned us, never said a thing until afterward and fingers started pointing. It didn't matter who it was. We learned the hard way there was almost no one we could trust in this country completely and we became much more watchful and careful, and we stuck it out. Lhey and I prayed and decided that if God had called us there it would be God who would decide when we would leave.

That same year I took over the administration of Nairobi Baptist Bible College in Ruiru town from Richard Konnerup. He and his wife, Ann, had gone home on furlough, and he asked me to look after the college. Ann was in poor health and when she was unable to return I continued with the college for the next eleven years. We had graduates who were starting churches and we worked with several of them. Richard taught me how to build a simple stone building with a ring beam and wooden trusses for the roof and I helped some of the men get started. We would also add an iron bar fence around the property and a married dormitory to the college campus.

In 2001 we put up a building for a church in an estate called Kihunguro. The work seemed to have started well but by the beginning of 2002 the pastor, one of our college graduates, suddenly quit. We had no graduates ready to take the church at the time, so we stepped in and I pastored my first church. We had thirty-one people the first Sunday but the Lord blessed and in six months we were building a larger auditorium and a parsonage for a future pastor, and on our first anniversary we set an attendance record of 205.

Kihunguro was a rural but growing area. Houses in the region were usually small with walls made of cut stones and tin roofs, often with unfinished plastering. But the people came, some walking a long distance. Charismatics also came trying to take control of our services. It was a battle all of our graduates faced. I learned early on that you have to screen people very carefully before you let them get involved.

I used an accordion for the music in our services and one Sunday a man came and told me that he could play the accordion and asked if he could play a special. I had a long talk with him about his salvation and baptism. He claimed to be a Baptist, so I had him audition a song. I figured if he joined us and could help with the music it would free me up in the service and at the time I could have used all the help I could get.

He could play all right, so I let him play us a special in the service. He played and sang, and when he finished he started preaching. I got up to tell him to stop and he started playing another song. When he finished he started preaching again. I got up to stop him and he started into another song and this time had the congregation join in singing with him. This time as soon as he finished I was on my feet and went up to him before he could start speaking again. Instead he said, "Let's sing another song." I told him no, it was enough and took the accordion off his shoulders. The next Sunday he came again and asked to play and I said no. We never saw him again.

We had a man named Charles, who was the cousin of one of our pastors and of one of our Bible college students. Charles was faithful to the church from the first Sunday we started. About six weeks later during the invitation at the end of the sermon, we were singing *Just As I Am*. Charles was sitting about half way back and on the first verse he stepped out into the aisle. On the second verse he moved up one row. On the third he moved up one more row. On the fourth he moved up to the second bench and I figured if we sang one more verse he might make it to the altar. We did and he did and when I asked him what he needed he said he wanted to be saved. Charles was our first convert in that church.

There are forty-two different tribal groups in Kenya. Most of them have modernized, taking English names and living in cities, but many of the tribes have remained primitive, living in mud houses in *manyattas* out in what we might call the boondocks in the States, but what they call the bush. Most of our work was in between. We were outside the big city in the country, but not so far as to be considered in the bush.

A *manyatta* is a small village with mud houses with grass roofs built in a circle often around one specific house that belongs to the patriarch of the tribe. Many of the surrounding houses will belong to his wives and the others to his sons. The sons will often take girls from nearby *manyattas* for wives, but there seems to be a lot of close relational marriages.

They fashion a thicket of thorns from acacia trees and build them up about ten feet high and surround the village with the brambles leaving one section for a gate that can be pushed out and in. This thicket is for protection from lions and other wild animals. When the mud houses are in need of repair they use cow dung to patch the walls. Inside a cook fire will be in the center with cowhide mats laid around to sleep on, and just inside the door a small cattle stall.

Most of these tribal people are cattle herders. They carry spears and wear red robes, supposedly because lions are afraid of red. They take their cattle out during the day and bring them in at night to the center of the village. The Masai love milk, and when they have a cow with a calf, they bring the calf into the stall in the mud house at night so that it can't drink it's mother's milk. In the morning the family will milk their cow and when they have what they need, they turn the calf out to feed on what's left. The most well known of these tribal people are the Masai, but there are many others, Pokot, Samburu, Rendille, Borani and more.

We had a young man named Joshua coming to our services. Shortly after Charles was saved he also came forward to trust Christ. Joshua was Rendille, but he spoke not only Swahili, but English as well. He had a friend named Rongai who spoke no English or Swahili. Now I preached occasionally in Swahili, but it took a long time to prepare, so I usually spoke in English and had an intern from the college interpret for me. Michael Mweru was doing his internship with the church and interpreting for me at the time. Joshua would sit in the back with Rongai and translate the message to him.

One Sunday Joshua brought Rongai forward and said he wanted to be saved. I told them to wait while we dismissed the service, and then I had Michael interpret the plan of salvation, and Joshua translate it to Rongai. Finally through the line of interpreters Rongai got the message from English to Swahili to Rendille clear and prayed to be saved.

It is interesting to me how the Lord blesses the efforts that we make in His service. One Saturday I went around the neighborhood visiting and I had six people promise me that they would come to the services the next day. Not one of the six showed up, but when the service started we had six other first time visitors.

We had a woman named Esther who had been faithfully attending and one of the six visitors was her husband, Joseph. The next Saturday when I went on visitation Joseph came to the church to go with me. We had visited a certain block of apartments and then he asked if we could visit a couple who were friends of his. "Sure," I said, and we dropped by their apartment.

After sharing the gospel with the couple they acknowledged their need and bowed their heads to pray with me.

When we were done I followed up with some verses about assurance of salvation. I told them, "Remember this date, because this is the day you have accepted the Lord." Joshua then piped up, "And me too. I prayed too!" I never saw the other couple again, but Joshua was faithful in church with his wife every week.

The ministry of course has its hardships and Kenya was no exception. The average lifespan in Kenya was only forty-seven. The average age of all living Kenyans was only fifteen, and the infant mortality rate was exceptionally high. One of our members, Grace, was saved the day we dedicated the first building with the original Kenyan pastor. She had one son who was five years old, but she had lost three others before they were six months old.

One evening just at dusk when Michael was visiting he found her hiding behind a gate at her apartment with a knife. Her husband, John, had been out drinking and she was so mad that she was about to attack him when he came home. Michael and his wife, Judy, talked with her for a long time and calmed her down. Then they arranged to visit her husband the next day. They shared the gospel with John and he gave his life to Christ and began coming to church.

Shortly after Grace gave birth to another boy and named him Daniel. He was a beautiful baby and she was so happy to have another child. We prayed long and hard for Daniel and when he reached his ninth month we were hopeful that this baby was going to make it, but at about ten months he suddenly died.

John and Grace were so poor that we paid the expenses at the morgue to collect the body. They couldn't even afford a casket so they put him in a dresser drawer and nailed a board over it. They don't embalm the bodies in Kenya unless you are wealthy enough to afford it. Otherwise they are kept in a freezer until they are claimed. When we picked up Daniel's body he was already thawing out, his face had turned red, and we took our last look at him before sealing the drawer and driving to the cemetery.

Cemeteries in Kenya are ghastly. They are not well kept with manicured lawns and flowers on all the graves with beautifully cut stone markers. We buried Daniel at the Nairobi cemetery on the south side of the city near the game park. The place was divided into two sections, one for adults and one for children. So many people are dying and being buried every day that they had row after row of graves already dug, and people lining up to bury their loved ones in the next available spot.

The children's side was the same way. In fact, we drove over a section of recently opened holes to the burial spot for Daniel. The graves were not deep, and they are only kept for five years. Then the remains are dug up and burned, and the plots are reused. The section we drove over had just recently been dug up. Fleas were everywhere and it was quite uncomfortable.

Grace was about the same size as Lhey, and when we finished the service she put her head on Lhey's shoulder and cried quietly. "I don't want to have any more children," she said. We were concerned that they might be discouraged and turn away, but the next Sunday they were both in church again and John gave to the offering for the first time.

We saw beggars all the time. People with leprosy would be left sitting on the sidewalks in Nairobi holding out fingerless hands asking for money. It's hard to walk away, but these people are brought there in the morning and taken home at night. Somebody takes care of them.

I don't like to give money when I don't know the background, but I would often buy food and give to them. One man sat in a wheelchair in a shopping district called Westlands\'. He was sitting at the corner of a parking lot every time I went into that area. So one day I bought him some food and gave it to him. He looked at me with a frown and not a word. When I had finished my business and walked by he had still not eaten the food. He never ate the food and was never thankful so I stopped giving him anything.

The saddest thing to see was the street kids. There were thousands of them in Nairobi and they hung out like gangs. In Ruiru we also had street kids hanging out around our little business district. There was a small grocery store where I bought the staples for the college and every week when I went there a group of street kids would be hanging around the door asking for money. They could be quite obnoxious.

There was a place in Thika, twenty minutes north of us, where we could buy eggs in bulk. One time when my mother was visiting we went for eggs and as we were coming out of the store eight or ten kids stuck their hands out for money. My mom took

Jonathan and hurried to the car, but that was her mistake. When she looked afraid the kids surrounded her all clamoring for money. I quickly opened the car and let Mom and Jonathan in, then loaded the eggs and got in the car. The kids didn't bother Lhey or me, but they got on the runners by the back door and pounded on the windows until I drove off.

The problem with giving money to these starving kids was that they used it to buy glue. A little bit in a small water bottle would last them for days and they would walk around holding it up to their noses. It put them in a stupor, eyes bloodshot, and looking half drunk, and they wanted nothing else.

I wouldn't give these kids in Ruiru money, but I would buy them each a box of tea biscuits to eat. They learned, and whenever they saw me coming they stopped asking for money and started asking for biscuits. Some of them would have a bottle of glue in their hand and try to hide it, but I knew who was using and I had one stipulation for them. Give me the glue and I'd give them the biscuits. They never would. Those poor kids were so addicted they wouldn't trade their glue for food to stay alive.

When people found out where we lived they started coming to our gate asking for money. The most common excuse was that their mother was in the hospital. They would usually say something like I'm a member at the Ruiru church and Pastor Christopher knows me, but I have this need. The church was next door to the college so I would tell them that I would be seeing Pastor Christopher the next day and I would ask him. If he told me it was a legitimate need then I would help. I never had one of those return.

One day a man came to my office at the college and told me that the Lord had told him that I would pay for the education of his children. I asked him, "Are you sure?" He said, Oh yes, the Lord had told him. I nodded my head and then told him, "Well, the Lord has told me I'm not." He smiled and left.

We had a lot of good students at the Bible college, but even some of them gave us trouble. One day a student came into my office and said he needed money to make an emergency trip home. His mother had died. I asked him which mother that was. He had told the same sad story to Richard Konnerup a couple years before. You would think they would try to be a little more imaginative.

One of the blessings of ministry is watching people grow spiritually. Moses and his wife Judith were saved and faithfully attended church. Moses was quite excited about learning the Bible. Every time we had a Sunday school contest he won. He learned all the memory verses and when I taught a series on the Romans Road and soul winning he determined to put it into practice.

One Sunday morning he came to church smiling from ear to ear and bringing a friend with him. When the morning worship began I asked Moses if he would like to give a testimony. "I sure would," he said enthusiastically. "I've been practicing what you taught us about soul winning and I shared it with my friend, Wycliffe, here, and this week he prayed and trusted the Lord, and I brought him to church." You just can't beat that kind of joy.

Chapter Five
The Comedy that is Life

I am convinced that many Kenyans have never had their heads under water because nearly every time I baptized in Kenya I had people who would panic when I put them under. Now as Baptists the only way we accept baptism is by immersion. It is immersion, going under, that pictures the burial, and the coming up that pictures resurrection (Romans 6:3-5), so there is no other method that is scriptural. Some may have people kneel down and just bend forward under the water, some have them sit and rock them back, while most often you'll find Baptists standing and the preacher laying the person down into the water. I don't think that the particular way it is done matters so much, but the idea of burial is important and that means getting under the water.

The first time I baptized in Kenya was in a swimming pool. From the start nearly every person I baptized that day, seventeen in all, had a panic attack. I baptize using my right hand behind the person's back. With my left hand I will hold the person's right hand by the wrist so that he or she can hold his or her own nose. Then with their left hand they hold onto my left forearm. If everybody holds on it works just fine, but inevitably the person going under the water got excited and started clawing at the air with the left hand, and opening the mouth about to hyperventilate, and then gulping a huge amount of water as they went under. I put them down and pulled them up as quickly as I could to minimize their water intake and choking.

We were helping one of our graduates named Kiarie start a new work in the mountains in a place called Ihindi. They were meeting in a barn on a country hillside. "Just follow the highway over the mountain until you see the sign. You can't miss it." How many times had I heard that? We didn't miss the sign along the highway, but finding his place was another story. He gave us no directions after the sign and we drove all over until we happened to find him on the road.

He wanted me to do the first baptismal service I think because it was his first church and he hadn't baptized anyone yet, and for another the baptistry was a muddy pond behind an earthen dam. I preached in the stuffy, dusty barn, and a spider bit Lhey, sitting on one of the benches. Her leg swelled up for several days.

The pond was not far away and we walked down to it, found a level spot on the bank and waded out into waste deep water. The bottom was soft, smooth mud. The first candidate was a man and as I put him down in the water my right foot slid out from under me until I nearly did the splits and my face was in the water. Lord, I thought, I'm going to lose this one.

I finally got a grip with my foot but was so off balance that I had to slide it back up bit-by-bit bringing the man up with me. He must have been under the water eight or ten seconds and I'm sure he was wondering if I was going to drown him. The ladies that followed were young and not so heavy but I was more cautious with them and didn't lose traction anymore, which was a good thing because nearly every one of them started clawing at the air and swallowing water when I put them under.

Kiarie ran into problems when the owner of the barn, who was an influential man in the area, wanted to control the church and began telling Kiarie what he could and could not preach. That was unacceptable so Kiarie started another work in a place called New Wood, which was much closer to our home, only a few miles north of the college. They were meeting in a schoolroom and Jonathan had learned a new song, *El Shaddai*, and wanted to sing for them. He gave his first solo special, and later when he learned to play the euphonium in his school band he played specials for us at Kihunguro.

Kiarie asked me to do his first baptismal service in New Wood also. We held this service in a small muddy river close by. It was also only about knee deep, but I couldn't see the bottom, so I walked carefully around feeling for a clear spot where I could lay down the baptismal candidates. Satisfied that it was clear I put the first man down right on top of a sharp pointed rock that struck the middle of his back. I had shuffled all around the rock and completely missed it. Quickly I pulled him toward me and put him down almost on my feet. I apologized to him all over when I got him up but he was a good sport about it. We adjusted our "baptistry" down stream after that, and I told Kiarie the next time he was on his own. I'd given him enough examples.

We had a baptismal tank at the Kihunguro church and as we prepared to use it for the first time we found it leaked. We had filled it up the day before but by the time church was over and we prepared to baptize the water level was barely above my knees.

Jonathan was the first candidate and I had the privilege of baptizing my own son. There was no problem getting him under as he was seven years old, but the next candidate was Joshua. I didn't realize until I hit his head on the side of the tank that we were too far over to the side and I had to kind of slide him to my left as I put him down below my knees to get him all under. He was all smiles when I apologized to him too. It didn't matter.

The people we worked with were so poor that sometimes in church they would bring vegetables from their gardens for the offering. They showed their appreciation for kindnesses that way too. One neighbor whom Richard Konnerup had helped with a matter came by one day and gave him an old rooster. He and Ann were about to leave on furlough. Our two houses were next to each other on three plots with storage sheds in the middle.

Richard didn't know what to do with the rooster so he suggested we build a hen house if we wanted and try to raise some chickens. Our worker, Sammy Kinyanjui, built the hutch, we got a chicken and the chicken laid nine eggs. They hatched and we had chicks going around the yard but we noticed they started disappearing. One night our German shepherd, Bronco, carried one in his mouth and very proudly laid it at our back door. We weren't too happy with him of course. But the bigger problem was a mongoose. It started carrying off the chicks one at a time.

Our night guard, Ezekiel, was a gentle giant. I think he had the same condition that the pro-wrestler Andre the Giant had. His face was big with an exceptionally large nose, his hands were huge and the soles of his feet curled around till they were almost on top of his feet. They were so big we could hardly find shoes that would fit him. His biceps looked like Arnold Schwarzenegger and his chest stuck out at the weirdest angle. He'd been in an accident once and his sternum was broken and never reset properly. It kind of pointed outward making his chest look even bigger.

He caught some thieves trying to steal a metal drain cover in front of our house and when we put the two teenage boys in the car to take them to the police post he hit each one of them in the back so hard I could feel it. Yet he was as meek and gentle as a person could be. He stuttered a lot in our presence and sometimes seemed helpless to do the simplest things.

Someone had given us a worn out trampoline that was so old the canvass hooks on the sides began wearing out and tearing. One day Ethan was on the trampoline and landed too close to the side. One of the straps broke and he slid down between the canvass and the frame and was hanging there strangling. Ezekiel looked at him, panicked, started shouting and running around in circles and did nothing till I got there and pulled Ethan out.

I was a little irate. "What's the matter with you?" I yelled. "Why didn't you just pull him out?" S-s-s-s sorry, Boss," he replied nervously. "I didn't know what to do?" It was an on the spot flash of anger on my part and I couldn't stay mad at Ezekiel. He really loved our boys and was distraught that he hadn't been able to help. But that was the end of the trampoline and he was quick to help me take it apart.

One morning we heard a lot of commotion over in the chicken pen. Ezekiel went running over and I came running out of the house. By then the commotion had ended but Ezekiel came running back to me stuttering, "M-m-m-m mango juice, m-m-m-mango juice." He had chased the mongoose off but I almost fell over laughing. "You mean mongoose?" I said. "Y-y-y-yeah, mongoose," he replied.

We finally had two chicks left. The rooster had killed the hen trying to impregnate it, and one of these chicks wasn't going to make it. It wasn't growing and it looked sick. Doctor Lhey took pity on it and spoon fed it some aspirin in water and tried to get it to eat, but it didn't matter. The next day the chick died. Not long after the rooster died and we figured there wasn't much point to the hen house. So we let the remaining chick grow up and then butchered it. It was the straggliest thing you ever saw and so tough we didn't want it so we gave it to Ezekiel. He thought it was heaven.

I told Sammy to tear down the hen house one day while I was at the college. When I got home that afternoon he had taken it all apart, cleaned up the yard and stacked the wood. He was about to go home when I noticed that his sky blue pants were an orange color. "What's that?" I asked him.

He was covered with chicken fleas. He brushed them off as best he could and went to get a *matatu* home. The next day I asked him how his trip was. He said he was sitting in the *matatu* and the people on either side of him start brushing their arms and scratching their legs. He said, "I wanted to scratch with them but I forced myself to sit still so nobody would guess where the fleas were coming from."

Many countries are known for their exotic foods, especially in the Orient, but nearly every culture has something of its own that is unique to the outside world. In Kenya it is called *ugali*. *Ugali* is a kind of a cake made from corn meal mixed with water and baked until solid. It kind of looks like angel food cake, but doesn't have the soft texture. It was more like eating a flavorless cake. If it was dry you could almost choke on it. If it was moist you could add it to anything and it wouldn't be too bad. It was just tasteless. The Kenyans would cook it in a bowl, flip it over, and cut a wedge out of the dome with a knife, then make a thumb impression in the middle and add whatever they we eating with it. We figured it got its name because when you first taste *ugali* you say, "Ooh, golly."

Most Kenyans suffered from dental decay and their teeth were often stained yellow. The result was very bad halitosis. When someone would come forward while we were singing during an invitation I would bend my head over and get my ear near their mouth to hear. Their breath was sometimes overwhelming. So on our first Father's Day we got gifts for all the fathers present; a toothbrush and a tube of toothpaste. When I pulled the first tube out of the bag to show the congregation all the wives cheered.

We worked with pastors in some pretty faraway places. Wilson Kibet built a church in the mountain town of Tinet. It was more like a village with only about three hundred people, and was spread all over the mountain at around nine thousand feet. It was a most beautiful lush green area with cool, clean air and magnificent views in every direction. The dirt road to the church was rugged and when it had rained it was hard to get up without four-wheel drive, but we loved going up to the church. You know you are in a far out place when the most exciting thing that happens to the kids all week long is to see a car go by. They would all run out by the side of the road and wave whenever we passed by.

One of our graduates, Obediah, started a work in a tea plantation town in the far west in a place called Nyamira. He had a congregation and asked if I would come out and look at a piece of property he was considering buying to put up a building. I made the trip with another missionary, looked at the property, spent the night and preached for him in the morning.

We stayed in the only hotel in town, a two story building along the main road that had small rooms barely wide enough for a single bed and a tiny bathroom, and a dining area above a bar and disco. At about ten o'clock, just as the drinkers were getting going in the bar, the power went out in the whole town. It was a clear night and I went out to look at the sky. We were so far out that there wasn't any ambient city light on the horizon in any direction, and looking to the sky there were more stars than you could almost imagine.

It reminded me of nights in the Philippines when I flew out over the South China Sea far enough to lose sight of any lights on the shore and turned off my cockpit lights. The canopy of stars in view from horizon to horizon at ten thousand feet in the pitch darkness was overwhelmingly magnificent.

"Ah Lord God," I prayed from Jeremiah 32:17. "Behold, thou hast made the heaven and the earth by thy great power and stretched out arm, and there is nothing too hard for thee."

About twenty minutes later we found out that the hotel had the only generator in the town. They turned it on and while everywhere else was dark the hotel lit up and the drinkers continued on. They sang karaoke, obliterating the words and melodies of dozens of songs until about 3 a.m. before things started to finally quiet down.

After church Obediah took us to what he said was the newest restaurant in town. It wasn't a new building, just a new business in an old place. There wasn't much on the menu so we all ordered chicken stew. I got a leg that was at least seven inches long in a plate of grease with a few tomato shavings in it. The skin on the leg was thick, yellow and cratered, and the meat underneath a dark purple color. I figured this chicken must have lived a long life to be that tall, and probably died several days ago. The meat was so tough that I couldn't peal it off with a fork. I couldn't even rip it off with my teeth when I tried to bite it. That chicken surely had rigor mortis setting in before it was even cooked. Everybody's chicken was the same so we all decided to do something safe and ordered chips (French fries). At least then all we had to worry about was the grease.

While we were eating some other folks came in and they also ordered the chicken stew. The cook with a meat cleaver then came over to a door beside where we were sitting and went into a back room. All at once we heard the "pock-pock-pocking" of an unhappy chicken and then a loud wham! While we watched the cook came back out with the headless chicken, dressed it and threw it into the pot without ever having drained the blood.

We were the only white people in town and before long a group of six boys were standing at the window staring in at us. My Land Rover was right behind them and I reached into my pocket for the key and hit the alarm. The horn went off and the lights flashed behind the kids and they all jumped up and ran away. Then one by one the crept up to the side of the car, moved to the front, and peered around at the headlights. I hit the button again and they all went running and laughing. This happened several times until we were ready to go.

In the car I had a box of Oreo cookies so I called the six boys to the back door and opened it up. Then it seemed like they came up out of the dirt. Instantly the six became over twenty. I handed each one an Oreo until I had one left. Then an old woman walking on a cane came by and stuck her hand out. I gave her the last one. The boys were all examining their cookies with strange looks on their faces. One boy finally asked me, "What do you do with it?"

"You eat it," I said.

His mouth dropped open. "You eat this?" he said incredulously. "Yes," I replied.

The old woman tried hers and when her eyes lit up and she smiled, nodding her head, the boys all ate theirs. Then they wanted more but I had emptied the box. Be grateful for what you have, I thought. An Oreo cookie was the greatest treat those boys had ever had.

I was working on a project with Ole Konnerup and one day we stopped for lunch at a local *hoteli*, a small restaurant. This place had only four tables and the cashier's counter in front. At the back of the room was a stainless steel counter and sink, and a window into the kitchen area behind it. We both ordered a stew and as I watched the cook came out from the back wearing an apron that looked like it hadn't been washed in over a month. On the floor in front of the sink was a rubber tub with dirty dishes sitting in water as brown as dirt. He took two plates out of the tub, splashed the dirty water on them to wash them off with his hand, and served our stew on those plates.

"You aren't going to believe what we're eating on," I said to Ole who had his back to the kitchen. "What you don't know won't hurt you," he said. "Yeah, but I know," I replied. Turned out it didn't hurt either one of us but Ole came down with typhoid several times in Kenya. I never did.

When a young woman in our church named Eunice asked me to perform her wedding I told her to bring the young man to the church so I could meet him and we would have some counseling together. She brought Robert over and I learned he belonged to a charismatic group. I questioned his salvation and he gave a good testimony of being saved. So I asked him, "If you marry Eunice are you going to take her away to your church?" "No," he said, "I'll come here."

The wedding day came and in the Kenyan tradition the bride goes to her parents home and the groomsmen go with the groom and try to coax her to come out. It can take awhile depending on how long the bride plays the game. She will act sad and frown all day so as to show sadness at leaving her parents home so they won't be offended that she is ungrateful. Eunice's home was two hours north almost to Nanyuki. The wedding was supposed to start at eleven, but the bridal party was nowhere to be found.

No matter, we knew they wouldn't be there on time, but Swahili time was worse than Filipino time. You expect someone to be thirty minutes to an hour late in the Philippines, but in Kenya it was usually more like an hour and a half to two hours. So we weren't expecting them right away, but when we got hold of them at about one o'clock that afternoon, they had just left Nanyuki. Two hours late already and two hours to go. We just waited. Food was being prepared and there was nowhere to go.

Robert's charismatic friends had come to set up a sound system. We had to run an extension cord across the street to an apartment building to get power, but they wanted to sing the wildest music and I told them no. I disconnected the whole thing, but I had no idea how many people would be coming. About three o'clock we talked to one of the groomsmen who said they'd had a flat tire but would be there soon. At four o'clock they showed.

Our auditorium was twenty-five feet wide and thirty-eight feet long. We'd had close to two hundred people in the auditorium before, but by the time they crowded in this day we had 280 packed in and standing, with an isle for the bridal party in the middle, and over a hundred more standing outside at the windows. I began to wish I had let them set up the sound system.

Twenty-three bridesmaids led the way doing a little two step forward, one step back shuffle and singing a song until they were all in and holding up flowers in an arch. The bride and the maid of honor came in and made their way to the front. Then everything was quiet. I said to our intern Michael, "We have a problem." He smiled at me like he didn't know what I was talking about. I said, "Where's the groom?"

"Oh!" he replied and went out to look. He found the groom and his nine groomsmen by the *choo* (outhouse). Apparently he was having cold feet. The groomsmen finally talked him into going in and we started. The ceremony went smoothly, but with all the guests there, when I came to my message, really a challenge to the bride and groom about marriage, I ad libbed my remarks into a message of salvation. It was a very simple lesson really, only fifteen minutes long with an invitation. There was no way to deal with people individually so I led in a general prayer. I could hear some voices mumbling so maybe some accepted the Lord.

Unbeknownst to me at the time was that there were five other preachers in the ceremony; three charismatic preachers, one Presbyterian pastor, and one Anglican bishop. All five of them said to me afterward it was the greatest message they'd ever heard. I thought surely you've heard better than this. It was only a simple fifteen-minute message, but I think it pointed out how shallow a lot of Christianity can be. We had seen charismatic preachers stick their finger in the Bible and hold it up saying, "The Bible says, the Bible says," but never quoting a verse or telling you what the Bible really says.

When we got to the ring ceremony I picked the smaller ring from the ring bearer to put on Eunice's finger and then realized it was too small. I was surprised because neither Eunice nor Robert was very big, but Eunice's fingers were actually bigger than Robert's. So I had to quickly switch them around.

They both seemed to be rather shy. When I pronounced them husband and wife and said you may kiss your bride Eunice got real stiff with her arms down by her sides and Robert looked panicked for a moment. Then he suddenly grabbed her by the shoulders and bounced her off his chest twice doing a cheek-to-cheek kind of hug. She was half stunned and he stood there with a sheepish grin on his face while the audience cheered. So we finally got them married, about five hours late, but Robert did start coming to our church.

Of course we had a lot of funerals. The first I preached for was a young woman of only thirty-eight years. She had an eight or nine year old daughter and after the service I spoke with the little girl. Her name was Leah. I told her my wife's name was also Leah and she cried.

The casket maker had not finished the casket when it was time for the funeral and the husband didn't want to wait around. So they got the body, put it in the casket and brought it to the church in the bed of a pickup truck. The casket maker rode along staining the wood as they came. He still wasn't finished at the beginning of the funeral service, so he waited until we were done and then continued painting the casket in the back of the truck on the way to the cemetery. He was determined to get it done and earn his pay.

I preached the funeral for another baby and on the way to the morgue to get the body the family wanted me to go around and pick up everybody they could think of. We wound up with twenty-two people, some of them large women, a lot of them small children, crammed into my Land Rover. There were so many that at the morgue we had to put the casket on the roof.

Kenyans are superstitious about death. They believe in what they call the "living dead." The spirits of the deceased hang around watching the family to make sure they are given the proper honor. The relatives live in fear of being haunted. This will go on for one generation or two until the ancestor is forgotten, but it is a continuous cycle. Nobody wants to deal with the dead and *matatu* drivers will charge exorbitant prices to transport a body somewhere.

Another superstition is that you have to be buried where you were born. That is your inheritance and your spirit must stay there. Of course, many people do not stay where they were born.

Jobs are elsewhere and they go where the work is, but if they die while away the family will do everything they can to bring the body home. This may not set well with neighbors if there was bad blood between people. The neighbors don't want to be haunted either.

Along with that some tribes like the Luhya believe that no one dies of natural causes. If someone dies it's because somebody has cursed him or her. As a result at the funeral the mourners wail and scream and cry making as big a scene as they can because if you happen to be there not making a big scene the family will believe you are the one who caused the deceased to die and they will come after you for revenge.

It also costs for some up to a year's salary just to get the body transported because few are willing to help. If the body had come from the freezer and not been embalmed the family would pack dry ice around the coffin and cover it with trash bags for the trip up country. We saw several of those wrapped up on top of *matatus* along the road.

Charles had been one of our most faithful members. He came to me one day with some paint that he donated to the church to paint the building. He wasn't feeling well, was quite congested, but I didn't realize how sick he was. Many people would come asking for help for a common cold, but Charles didn't ask for anything. So it was a shock when three days after bringing the paint he suddenly died. He was in a *matatu* with his wife going to Nairobi to the hospital when he breathed his last. As soon as the people in the van realized he had died they started screaming. The driver pulled over and they put the body out on the side of the road. His wife begged them to take them to the top of the hill they were on, only about three hundred yards where there was a police post, but the driver refused.

We often counseled our people to do themselves a favor and bury their dead close by so that they didn't strap themselves with impossible debts for years to come. But in Charles's case, he had been so faithful that we decided to help the family by paying to send his body up country. A group from our church including Sammy, Michael, Esther, and Namaan went along with Pastor George Situma and one of our students, Martin Wangila. George and Martin were brothers, and cousins of Charles.

Charles' family belonged to an anti-Christian, anti-white cult group called the *Masambwa*. It was decided it would be best if I didn't go.

They held the funeral service on the family plot in the open air. The father refused to attend, and Charles' wife was not allowed by his family to attend. She sat under the banana trees off to the side. We found out then that Charles and Jennifah had never legally been married. They were both widowed and just started living together, but Charles had never paid a dowry for her so the family didn't recognize her or her children as legitimate heirs. As it turned out Charles also had a twin brother that we didn't know about. He didn't attend the funeral either because of a superstition that if a twin sees his sibling dead he will die in the same manner soon.

George led the service and was preaching when a group of *Masambwa* started up the hill from behind with a drum and making a lot of noise. They marched in line right into the middle of the funeral service. Charles had a sister who was quite large and she wasn't going to sit still for it. She grabbed the drum, tossed it into the trees, and then tackled the player and began throttling him. Then it turned into a melee.

Someone kicked Charles' sister and she ran into the woods. Namaan, who was as skinny as a ski pole ran into a cornfield and hid behind a stalk. George, who wasn't much bigger than Namaan stood his ground and kept saying, "Peace, brothers. Peace." No one bothered him, but another brother, Henry, had his skull split open when someone hit him with a board from behind, and Martin was under attack. Martin was big with broad shoulders and not one to be trifled with. He grabbed two of the *Masambwa* and knocked their heads together, and then he cold cocked several others. When the man with a board came up behind Martin, Charles' sister came roaring back from the woods and tackled him. Every now and then Namaan stood up and looked over the corn stalk and then ducked behind it again. Eight *Masambwa* lay unconscious on the ground around Martin and the remainder fled. Then the police showed up and stayed to maintain the peace until the funeral was over.

I asked Namaan what he was doing hiding behind a corn stalk in the field. He just smiled and said, "Look at me. I can't do anything."

But he could pray. Namaan was not one of our brightest students at the college. He'd never finished high school, but he was certain God had called him to preach so we gave him a chance and let him enroll. He never made high grades but he studied and wouldn't give up. He did his internship at our Kihunguro church.

I liked to keep a tight schedule and tried to be done by noon each Sunday. I also told the interns when they preach that they had thirty minutes. I know content is important, but I don't think a message accomplishes much if it goes too long and the listeners get bored.

One Sunday morning I scheduled Namaan to preach. I was amazed at him. The message was excellent and he got right at it. Then all of a sudden at noon straight up he quit. He had only preached for fifteen minutes and I knew he had more. I asked him why and he said he was trying to be done at noon. It illustrates how easily miscommunications like that happen when dealing with other languages. I appreciated what he did, but I didn't give him the pulpit until 11:45 and I told him next time to take the thirty minutes.

Namaan and his wife and babies lived in an apartment block not far from the church. We never held Sunday evening services in the area because there was very little lighting and gangs roamed the area at night so we didn't want our people to feel obligated to be out. One night a gang of thieves broke into the compound where Namaan lived. There were seven apartments in a row with a high stonewall around the courtyard. Namaan lived in the last apartment at the far end from the gate. The gang hit the first apartment, smashed in the door, ransacked it and went to the next. They came right down the block breaking into every apartment.

Namaan locked the door and windows and sat down with his wife and prayed. He told me later he didn't know what he would have done if they had broken in. He couldn't have fought them. So they just prayed as they heard the thieves getting closer. Finally they were at their door, pounding and saying let us in. Namaan took a deep breath and yelled back as loud as he could, "Go away!" They did. His was the only apartment that didn't get broken into.

In September 2010 our German shepherd, Bronco, died. He was one-eighth black Labrador, so he had more black than gold hair and his face was slightly wider than a pure shepherd, but he was a beautiful dog. He seemed to be a sensitive dog too. We also had a white mutt named Snowy who hated to get a bath. Bronco sat stoically through his baths but Snowy fought tooth and nail and when we finally got him pinned down he just whimpered. Bronco would come over and nuzzle him as if to try and comfort him.

The two dogs had quite opposite personalities. Bronco loved fireworks; Snowy was scared to death. Every New Years Eve we would get fireworks and set them off to celebrate. When a string of firecrackers would go off Snowy ran yelping, but Bronco stood over the firecrackers barking and snapping at the string of explosions.

One year we found a firecracker called a Gorilla Monster Bomb. It was huge. I set it up in the middle yard and not knowing what to expect we all got behind the gate so we could duck if we had to. I tried to keep Bronco inside, but when I lit the fuse he forced his way into the yard when I came through the gate. He stood over the monster bomb barking until it went off, a low, dull, boom that was so loud we felt the percussion thirty feet away as it echoed all around the neighborhood. Bronco stood there looking down, frozen in place, mouth open, not moving. I don't know if he was unconscious on his feet or just in shock, but I ran over to him calling his name and then started massaging his sides and neck and rubbing his head. He finally came out of it.

He had been sickly for about six months, eating very little, and had gotten really thin, but one night when I gave him some water and he threw it up I figured his time was short. I told Jonathan in the morning to say goodbye to him because I didn't know if he'd still be there when he got home from school. Sometime that afternoon he passed away while Ezekiel was watching. We buried him under the tree in our front yard that evening and Ezekiel said, "I'll be next because Bronco loved me."

We didn't think anything of it, but a month later I was in my office on a Saturday afternoon when Lhey came running into the house shouting Ezekiel had fainted. I ran down the stairs and out to the guardhouse. His daughter, Miriam, came out crying and I began to expect the worst. Ezekiel had collapsed on the floor and was half sitting up against a bookshelf. His eyes were half open and empty. I called his name and tried to sit him up and as I lifted him a grunt came out from his lungs. I thought there might still be a chance.

Ezekiel weighed 240 pounds so Jonathan helped me carry him out on the porch where we could stretch him out on the ground. When we laid him down there was another grunt of air so I tried CPR for about ten minutes but he was already gone. I went and got Sammy and Pastor Christopher Ochieng, who was the pastor of the largest church we worked with which was in Ruiru next to the college, and we went to the police post to make the report.

The only question the police wanted to know was whether or not Sammy and Christopher thought I had killed Ezekiel. No, of course not, they said. Two policemen came to the house and did a quick investigation, and after they filled out their paperwork we took Ezekiel's body to the Kenyatta University mortuary and had him embalmed. The process only cost eighty dollars and Ezekiel had worked with us for almost twelve years so we figured it was worth it for the family's sake.

His brother Jocabu, the police captain, another brother and his sister, Ruth, came to our house and we made the plans to send his body home for the funeral. Of course, we bore all the expenses. Jocabu for all his accomplishments was still typically very superstitious. When we went to view the body at the mortuary he leaned over Ezekiel's face and said, "You must leave, you can't stay here." He was speaking to his spirit.

We bought a suit for Ezekiel but they didn't want to put on shoes. The superstition is that heaven is a holy place and you can't enter wearing shoes. We wanted to be as accommodating as we could without surrendering to superstition, and since the lower portion of the casket was closed and nobody would see his feet I figured the shoes didn't matter.

When they wanted to take off the tie I decided to make a stand. They wanted to take off the tie because another superstition says that if he is wearing a tie the spirit can't leave the body. I told them Ezekiel was a Christian and his spirit was already gone. Still they insisted so we came up with a compromise. We loosened the tie around his neck but left it on. They accepted that.

The question then became what to do with his remaining children. He had two daughters, one was nineteen, and the other thirteen, and a granddaughter who was six that he took custody of when both of her parents died of AIDS. The family wanted us to take care of them and we agreed to do what we could. We put the oldest, Miriam, through a sewing class, bought her a Singer sewing machine and set her up in a business. We sent the second daughter, Brenda, to a boarding school and paid her expenses until she graduated three years after we left Kenya. The youngest was named Mercy. We took care of her until we left and Ezekiel's youngest son, Kennedy, who had two other young children, took her in.

We held a service at the mortuary and then they took the body in a modified van hearse and traveled to the home place in Kitale in western Kenya. Ezekiel was well known by many of our workers and pastors, and several people from the church went along for the funeral including Pastor Christopher and Sammy.

Ezekiel was very popular among his neighbors and when they heard he had been embalmed everybody around came to view the body because they had never seen one embalmed before. But there was one neighbor right next door who had been at odds with Ezekiel and at midnight the crowd of mourners got riled and decided to burn his house down. Sammy and Pastor Christopher got in front of the rowdies and while they waited for the police to come calmed the crowd down, and then Christopher preached to them. The Spirit of God worked and many people, angry only minutes before, were suddenly on their knees asking God to save them.

We finally got Ezekiel buried but we weren't done with him yet. There was another superstition that after forty days they had to send a witchdoctor to the place where the deceased had died to drive away his spirit. People are enslaved to this living dead idea. Jocabu insisted on sending a witchdoctor. We told him no, but he being a police captain had the power to force the issue and he was threatening to do it. I finally had Sammy tell him that if he came with a witchdoctor and forced us to let him in that he would have to take Ezekiel's daughters with him when he left because we would not take care of them.

I wouldn't really have done that, but I called his bluff and we heard no more about it.

The real blessing of ministry is seeing people respond and growing in their faith. We had a night guard at the college named Joseph who was on his annual leave when I took over for Richard Konnerup. Joseph was late returning from his vacation, but on the second day he called and said his money had been stolen and he was on his way.

Joseph had two sons, Stanley and Zakayo. Stanley was a very energetic boy, and while a little plump, he could run like the wind. He was always smiling and he would come up to me and try to surprise me with his sometimes audacious activities.

Whenever it rained these giant flying ants would come out of the ground. The rain would beat off their wings and these big old things, sometimes an inch long or more, lumbered around on the ground and were easily scooped up. The Kenyans liked to fry them and eat them. One day Stanley came into my office with a live ant between his fingers, walked up to me, and stuck the ant into his mouth and ate it with a big smile on his face, and then ran out the door.

We also had plenty of trouble with termites and whenever we found a colony we would dig it up until we found the queen. Termite queens were another delicacy and whenever we found them we tried to capture them live so the workers could fry them for another snack. The trick was to get them out and avoid the soldier termites that protected them. They were four times the size of the little monsters that eat up all the wood and have red heads and big mandibles. I've been bitten and it hurts.

Zakayo was the opposite of Stanley. Their mother had died and he was very quiet and introverted. When Joseph returned from his leave he brought with him a new wife, Josephine. She took care of the boys as if they were her own, and seemed to give Zakayo new life.

The following year Joseph was late returning from his leave again with the same excuse, his money had been stolen from his pocket while he was asleep on the bus. The third year the same thing happened, only Joseph didn't call, and when he was over two weeks late and the school term was about to start, I hired a new night guard. Two days later Joseph reappeared at the college. Joseph had worked for Richard for several years and Richard asked me if I could find some work for him to do. I made him the gardener and moved him into an unused classroom until we finished construction on a married dormitory and gave him a room there. He turned out to be a better gardener than he was night guard and I kept him on as long as I ran the college.

Joseph was always complaining about medical problems. He had a hernia, he had congestion in his lungs, every time I turned around he said he had malaria. That was not uncommon, however. Malaria, although it is the leading scourge in all of sub-Saharan Africa, is also the disease of choice of quack doctors in the countryside. Whenever someone got sick the first diagnosis was malaria. Even if it was just a common cold, they called it malaria.

The treatment for malaria is quinine. You poison the virus. The problem was that the country doctors would prescribe quinine for little babies that had nothing more than a runny nose and give them adult strength doses. I think if a study could be done they would find those doctors contributed greatly to the infant mortality rate.

I collected a stock of Panadol (Tylenol), peroxide and cotton, Band-Aids, cold tablets, and other things for minor medical needs, and told all the students to come see me first whenever they weren't feeling well. Usually a few pain pills or cold tablets settled the problem. But when Stanley got sick while we were on furlough a quack doctor decided he had kidney problems and put him on prednisone, another adult strength medicine. When we got back we took Stanley to Gertrude's Garden, a children's hospital, to see Jonathan's doctor and he put him on a schedule to get him off of the prednisone. He spent several days in the hospital, but when the medicine ended he was well again and came home.

Unfortunately, the next time we were out of the country and Stanley wasn't feeling well again, Joseph took him back to the quack doctor, who tried to take a biopsy of his kidney, but missed with the needle and had to do it again. It all became infected and Stanley in great pain very quickly faded and died.

Joseph was always complaining of a cough. I confronted him about smoking, which at first he denied, but then later confessed to me that he was doing. I told him I wasn't going to help him if he didn't stop smoking. Faced with the option he finally broke the habit. In 2006 I expanded the college to include a one-year Bible Institute program and opened enrollment for anyone in our churches. We met one day a week and Joseph asked me if he could attend. I was skeptical at first because he overall hadn't been real trustworthy, but I enrolled him.

He studied hard, did well, and Josephine told Lhey later that the change in his personality was phenomenal. He took to heart everything he was learning and applied it. He became faithful in his church and eventually became so respected for his honesty that he was elected a deacon and became the church treasurer.

The Lord eventually blessed Joseph and Josephine with two more children. The first was a daughter. The day Josephine's water broke she went to the hospital close by, but her contractions were not strong yet so they told her to go for a walk and come back. She walked back to the college and tried to sleep, but when the contractions got stronger she couldn't get back to the hospital in time and the baby was born at the gate between the college and the church.

In Kenya names often have to do with the circumstances of the birth. Joseph wanted to name the baby *Nangila*, which means "in the way," but Josephine didn't like it. They couldn't agree on a name, so Lhey told them that when our first child was coming we had decided on Shannon if we had a girl. They both liked the name so she was named Shannon *Nangila*.

About a year later Josephine was expecting another child, but the baby was late coming. When she was nearly a month overdue we took her to the Kenyatta University hospital where they induced labor and she gave birth to a boy. We had paid all the expenses, of course, so in gratitude they named the boy Lance *Sudi*, *Sudi* being a traditional family name. So I have a namesake running around Kenya!

Chapter Six
The Grace of God

When Jonathan was born Lhey had a very hard labor complicated by the doctors leaving her in labor for twenty-five hours until they finally decided a C-section was necessary. In the surgery Lhey's heart began to fail from fatigue and her right lung collapsed. Then Jonathan struggled to breathe for the first few moments until they suctioned his nose and throat three times. To make it worse they gave Jonathan an IV in his left hand but missed the vein. When they saw it some time later his hand was swollen to the point it looked like the skin would break. They packed his hand in ice and his hand recovered but it left a large scar on the back of his hand.

I was there watching in the surgery. They put a chair by Lhey's pillow so I could sit with her, but she was out and they had a sheet blocking my view and I couldn't see so I stood up. One doctor quickly told me there would be a lot of blood and maybe I should sit. I said, "I'll be okay." I had investigated one fatal Naval aircraft accident. The blood wasn't going to be anything compared to what I had seen. And it wasn't.

Lhey was in the hospital ten days and was so weak she was unable to hold Jonathan until he was two days old, and then only for a minute. Her heart was enlarged and it took her a long time to recover. The ladies at our church, South Sheridan Baptist, were wonderful in helping her clean the house and bringing over meals. In five months her heart had returned to normal, but we decided to put off having more children for a while.

After a year or so we stopped taking precautions but no more children came and we had concluded that Jonathan was going to be an only child. Then in May 2007, almost thirteen years later, Lhey was expecting again. When we went to Kenya we had decided that if Lhey ever did conceive again we would go home to have the baby in the States but very quickly, as we used to say in the Navy, that plan was OBE (overcome by events).

When Lhey tested positive we went to see an Indian gynecologist that several missionaries recommended, Dr. M.D. Patel. He ordered an ultra sound and we saw the egg and the yoke sack. Several days later on a Sunday morning Lhey had spotted some blood so we decided to go to the hospital as a precautionary measure.

The Nairobi Hospital is in the center of the city not far from the parliament buildings. Dr. Patel's office was just down the street and it was the most convenient hospital with him attending. It was, however, a long drive for us living twenty kilometers, about twelve and a half miles north of the city center. Lhey wasn't feeling badly and on the way to the emergency room she was hungry and we stopped to get something to eat. At the hospital she had an ultra sound, by now the baby was a little blob about the size of my thumbnail. They could find nothing that was the cause of the bleeding and she was fine.

About ten days later the story changed. Lhey woke me up at one-thirty in the morning and said, "I'm bleeding." Being the dutiful husband that I am I said, "Can it wait until morning?" She said more emphatically, "No, I'm bleeding."

I quickly jumped up, turned on the light, went around the bed and found her sitting on the floor in a pool of blood. She was hemorrhaging. At that point I thought she had lost the baby and my first concern was that she was bleeding to death. I woke up Jonathan, wrapped Lhey in some towels, and we very delicately carried her down the stairs to the car.

We lived on a very bad dirt road and I drove so slow that the speedometer never came off zero, but she still felt every bump and cried out in pain. It was a mile to the highway, but the highway was so full of potholes that it wasn't much better. I never got faster than thirty miles an hour and the trip to the hospital which normally would have taken forty minutes at night with no traffic took an hour and a half.

We finally got her to the emergency room at Nairobi Hospital and a Kenyan doctor came to check on her. After his examination he said the pregnancy is over. Jonathan looked at me and asked, "What did he say?" I said, "The baby's gone." I don't know who shed the most tears just then but we hugged each other and just wept. Lhey very stoically watched us with misery in her eyes, but no tears. She was handling it better than we were.

I went out to check her into a room and when I came back the doctor was preparing to work on her. "What we'll do now," he said, "is called a D and C Procedure." Now I had been supporting National Right to Life for nearly twenty years and I knew a D and

C was a method of performing an abortion. I incredulously asked the doctor, "Is the baby still there?"

He said, "There is evidence of fetal material but it can't survive."

I asked him again if the baby was still there. He gave me the same answer, "There is evidence of fetal material but it can't survive."

I told him in no uncertain terms that he wasn't doing anything more until we had an ultra sound done. We got Lhey checked into a room and then waited. It was 4 a.m. Dr. Patel arrived at the hospital at nine and after looking over the report very kindly talked to us about God's will and sometimes He has other plans for us. We were very grateful for his sincerity and understanding. It was reassuring even though he was not a Christian.

The ultra sound technician finally came at ten and we wheeled Lhey to the exam room and did the procedure. He found the baby, about an inch long, and we could see his heart. He had the volume on but I was so certain we were going to find the baby dead that I didn't even hear it and I was about ready to comfort Lhey when the technician said, "The baby is fine."

"What?" I was shocked. Jonathan gave me a strange look and said, "Didn't you hear the heart beat?" I said no, so the technician turned the machine back on, turned up the volume, and did it again and there it was, pounding, alive and healthy. Talk about joy from despair.

What happened was the placenta had attached very low in the birth canal and had torn loose. That's where the blood came from. It was hanging almost literally by a thread. Dr. Patel said this kind of condition rarely survives. Lhey was in the hospital for another ten days before she could come home, and when they checked her out Dr. Patel ordered her to be on total bed rest. He didn't have to worry. She developed such a bad sciatic nerve pain she hardly wanted to move from the bed.

Jonathan's school was nearly an hour away and I had the college to look after, so we arranged to bring Lhey's sister, Rachel, over from the Philippines to help look after her. Once a month we went back to the hospital for a check up and ultra sound. It was the most beautiful thing I have ever seen watching the baby grow to two inches, then six, the legs and arms stretch out and the head begin to take shape.

Since we had a son several friends and relatives were hoping we'd have a girl, but Jonathan wanted a brother because he wanted to call him "Bob." When the baby was big enough the ultra sound revealed a boy. We had gone from the hospital to Jonathan's school to pick him up. He was playing soccer when I called him over to the car. He was all nervous about the result. Then I told him, "I have to tell you that you'll be able to call him 'Bob.'" A huge smile came over his face and he started shouting, "Yes!" Then he ran off to tell all his friends at soccer practice that he was having a brother.

As it turned out, Ethan's due date was January 14, the exact same day Jonathan was born, but that too would change. In October in the sixth month, Lhey had some bleeding again and when we had the ultra sound we saw the baby lying flat on his back. Then all at once his face turned toward us and he raised his right arm and swung his hand back and forth like he was waving at us. We imagined him saying to us, "I'm okay." Lhey spent a couple more nights in the hospital and was fine. Years later I told Ethan the story and he said, "Yeah, I remember that!"

Then on December 11, Lhey bled some more. We went to see Dr. Patel and he suggested it was time to birth the baby before she lost him, which turned out to be a fortunate decision. We checked Lhey into the hospital and the doctor gave her a steroid injection to help the development of the lungs and scheduled the birth for the fourteenth. That night Lhey hemorrhaged again. It was decided she couldn't wait three more days, but the earliest they could reserve the theater was on the thirteenth.

I went direct to the hospital that morning after dropping off Jonathan at school. Dr. Silverstein, an American heart specialist at the hospital who had been former President Moi's personal physician, had checked Lhey's heart a couple months earlier. This morning he came by to see her and said he would be standing by in the event of an emergency. He was very comforting as well.

Dr. Patel had put together a team of physicians for the surgery; His wife, Dr. D.M. Patel, was the anesthesiologist, a surgeon, Dr. A.L. Patel, and a pediatrician named Dr. Atul Patel were also there. Only M.D. and D.M. were related. (Patel in India is as common as Smith in America.) I wasn't allowed in but I was standing at the door and when I heard the baby cry I knew everything was going to be all right. I had given blood in advance and it was a good thing because they needed two units in the surgery, but Lhey was also healthy, no heart problems this time.

Lhey and Ethan were in the hospital for ten more days. She had a private room, which turned out to be the presidential suite. Because our insurance was a group plan with the mission, we looked at getting a semi-private room to save costs, but they didn't have a place prepared for Lhey until after Jonathan and I had gone home. What they took Lhey to was a disaster for her. It was a ward with dozens of other women and her semi-private room was a corner with a curtain around it. It had a public restroom that everybody used and she had no private nurse to help her get to it. It was not air-conditioned and it smelled.

We didn't leave Lhey with her cellphone afraid it might get stolen, so she had no way to call me, but she immediately complained she couldn't stay there and wanted to go back to the presidential suite. Unfortunately someone else had already scheduled it, but just as Lhey was about to despair the other people decided they couldn't afford it, so the nurses were able to take her back up to the room. When I arrived the next day I decided the cost didn't matter, I'd make it up if I had to myself, but she was staying in the presidential suite. (Our insurance covered it.)

The suite was nice and had a TV with one channel that played the same six Pink Panther cartoons over and over all day. The food they prepared for her was more than she could eat, so I would pick up Jonathan every afternoon from school and we would go to the hospital and help Lhey eat her dinner. Ethan was in an incubator for several days but he grew strong quickly. He looked like Jonathan's identical twin at birth.

We brought them home on December 23 just in time for Christmas, and then the whole ordeal began to make sense. Sometimes when you go through the trials you wonder what in the world God is trying to do. In this case it became clear.

Kenya held presidential elections on December 28, 2007. The Kenyans had a reputation for being one of the calmest of nations on the continent when it came to elections. There had never been a civil war, although there had been one failed coup attempt, but very little unrest and violence in past elections. This time it changed.

The two candidates, Kibaki and Odinga had fought very hard campaigns and the voting was close. While the outcome was still in question Odinga, trying to pre-empt and influence the final decision, declared himself the winner and began parading around town with a large crowd of supporters celebrating. But Kibaki, the incumbent, wasn't going to let it go that easy, and sometime after midnight the final count put him in the lead. About four days later the Supreme Court announced that Kibaki was the winner.

What erupted was a tribal conflict that had been magnificently held in check for decades. Now it broke open. Kibaki was a Kikuyu, the largest tribe; Odinga a Luo, the second largest tribe. The two tribes hated each other and battles between the two tribes plus the Kalengin and others broke out all over western Kenya. In Nairobi a blood cult gang called the *Mungiki* blocked the highway near the Mathari slum where the highway leaves the city going north, and rioting at the Githerai roundabout, the same one where my car had been stoned, blocked all traffic going south into the city.

The alternative way to Nairobi was to go through Ruiru, where the college is, and around the north side of the city. In the Ruiru area the Kikuyu are dominant. The Kenyatta family owned a milk company that was a couple of miles north of our house. When the Luos in the west burned down one of the milk company branches, the Kikuyus in Ruiru attacked the minority Luos in town. The Luos fled to the prison on the west side of town where the warden was a Luo and set up a tent city on the grounds.

Sammy called me and said don't come out here. People are just wandering about the streets and fights are breaking out all over. It's not safe. I agreed and stayed home.

I had stocked up on food and water just in case and it was a good thing I did, but I hadn't anticipated the length of the conflict. We were stranded for eleven days before it ended, and right in the middle of those eleven days was Ethan's due date. If Lhey hadn't suffered, had gone full term and Ethan hadn't come early, they both would likely have died because I'd never have been able to get them to the hospital.

Chapter Seven
The Filipino Call

We always traveled through the Philippines on our way to Kenya and back home to visit Lhey's family and had many ministry opportunities there. They always had me speak in the church in Olongapo, and on one visit to the northern part of Negros in the town of Victorias, Lhey's *Tiyay* (Aunt) Judith had arranged for me to speak at the local high school. While I was speaking to the senior class Lhey, her sister Rachel, and their cousin, Rowena, went out in the school courtyard and started witnessing to students on breaks.

When I was finished I went and joined them at a table, but there was one fellow that kept interrupting Lhey as she spoke. "What is your authority for speaking?" he asked. I tried to make him be quiet but he kept speaking up. "You have to have a proper authority. You can't speak without it." Judith had joined us with her Bible in hand. She was all of four foot nine inches, but a giant in the faith. When she had enough of the young man she set her Bible on the table, put her finger on the cover and said very emphatically, "Our authority is the Word of God. There is no other." Judith is what Filipinos often call "small but terrible!" The kid went away and didn't bother us anymore.

I found him later and talked with him. He belonged to a charismatic cult group called The Apostles of the Fourth Watch. They claimed to have a direct line of succession back to the Apostles and only someone who was in that direct line had authority to teach the Bible.

We found many Filipinos in Kenya who were there on work visas, mostly in garment manufacturing, but in other professions also. One was married to the Swiss director of the Red Cross in Kenya. All of the accountants for the Red Cross were Filipinos. The director told me they didn't trust Kenyans with any job handling money so they hired accountants from the Philippines.

The Philippine ambassador, Libas, loved to socialize and everything from Philippine Independence Day to staff birthdays was an occasion for *lechon* (roast pig) and a party. Every occasion began with a mass. The Filipino priests would come with their accouterments in a little brief case, set up on a table, do their ceremony, and when they were through, blow out the candles and put all the items away, take off their robes, and get a beer. We tried to time our travel to the embassy to arrive after the mass was done.

On our first Independence Day visit the mass was finished, the party was on, and when the *lechon* was ready the consul, Julius Caesar Flores, asked one of the priests to pray. He stood at the front of the line and said, "Let's attack." He grabbed a plate and started. Flores was not a little disappointed.

The party went on all day and there was plenty of food left over, so at about 6 p.m. they put the food out again and the consul asked another priest to pray. He said that we had already prayed and didn't want to. Lhey overheard the conversation and told Julius that I could pray, so he asked me. I said sure, gathered everybody around and unlike the formula prayers from a book that the priests used, I prayed, thanked the Lord for Jesus Christ who shed His blood to pay for all of our sins, who is the way the truth and the life, and the only means of salvation by faith in Him alone.

When I was done Julius said to me, "You pray like a professional." I asked him, "What do you mean?" He said, "You sound like you are actually talking to someone, like you know what you're doing, not just reading it from a book." Imagine that.

The embassy really made our ministry international. The door was open to share the gospel with diplomats as well as foreign workers from Switzerland, Holland, France, Germany, and Thailand. One of the embassy staff had a birthday party at her apartment swimming pool. We were invited and at the party was a Thai diplomat named *Nut*. He asked Julius what Christianity was all about, and Julius called me over to explain it.

We talked for the next hour and *Nut* showed great interest. I started in Genesis 1:1 and explained the Bible to him, creation, the fall of man, the promised Savior, and the fulfillment in Christ. Finally *Nut* said to me, "Yes, I believe Jesus is God."

I said, "Would you like to accept Jesus as your Savior?" "No," he replied. "I believe Jesus is God, but there are many gods."

It illustrates the difficulty of reaching people in non-Christian cultures. Unfortunately, although I met Nut on two or three other occasions, I never had another chance to have a long conversation with him.

On Jonathan's birthday in 2001 we invited several Filipino families to our house for a party. We lived on the opposite side of Nairobi from the embassy a long way out and it wasn't easy to find our place, but a few people came. After eating I sat with them under our *bonda*, a picnic table around a center post with a grass roof, in the yard and shared the gospel with them. The Swiss Red Cross director pulled his sunglasses down over his eyes and took a nap sitting up. He would tell me on another occasion that he believed in reincarnation.

His Filipino wife argued with me constantly, but another Filipina, Miriam, who was also married to a Swiss man who had just died, listened intently, asked a lot of questions, and after a few more visits with her she gave her life to the Lord.

While I was talking another Filipino named Moley had tears in his eyes, and Lhey invited him to go into the kitchen so they could talk. He had been living with a Kenyan woman while his wife was back in the Philippines. He prayed and repented and immediately afterward moved out from the woman's apartment. Lhey met the woman on another occasion and spoke with her. She was very nice but would not accept the Lord. Moley was determined to salvage his marriage and in a few months he went home to reconcile with his wife.

In the meantime he moved in with a Kenyan friend of his named John Mwangi. One day he brought Mwangi out to our house and I shared the gospel with him under the same *bonda*. Mwangi had grown up in an orphanage and was a tout on a *matatu*. He was a rough guy like they all were, but as we talked the tears came to his eyes and he gave his life to Christ.

Moley told us the transformation in his life was for real. They went home and he immediately started sharing what he had done with their landlord. They lived in a town called Ongatta Rongai, more than an hour from our home, but they came up every Sunday to go with us to church and some days during the week to learn more, and Mwangi began witnessing to his tout friends. On New Years Eve they came over and brought Mwangi's sister, Ann, and a cousin, and after a long evening of sharing they also accepted the Lord.

We were blessed to see many in the Filipino community come to the Lord but events in 2004 started to turn our thoughts back to the Philippines. In 2004 the Kenyan government imposed a tax on expats that in the past had always exempted missionaries. This time we were included. We spent months fighting it, appealing to all levels of the government, even trying to get the U.S. Embassy to help.

The embassy asked me to find out how many Protestant missionaries were in the country (Catholics were not held liable for the tax.), how many nationals they employed and how many people they worked with. I contacted every organization I could find, found there were more than 1500 missionaries of all denominations in the country, employing over 10,000 Kenyans directly and ministering to over a million people not only with churches and schools but hospitals, medical clinics, and in digging wells.

On December 21, 2004 I called my contact at the embassy and asked where I needed to turn in this information. She told me the embassy would be closed for the holidays and to contact them back after the New Year. The next day the embassy sent out an email to all missionaries stating the Kenyan tax law, that we were required to pay, and offering contacts with tax lawyers to help us. They didn't even consider the information I had gathered or our appeal, and when I complained to them I got an email back explaining the above and asking me why I thought they hadn't helped. Yeah, I wonder why I would think that.

By the way, the Kenyan tax code had been revised with the help of the United States IRS.

Those who could afford to pay signed up, but many missionaries left the country, and we decided to make a survey trip to the Philippines to see if the Lord was leading us in another direction. We arrived at our old home church in Olongapo and I preached in a citywide crusade they were hosting, but two weeks after our arrival the pastor resigned and the deacon committee asked me to take the church. Since we were planning to go back to Kenya if the tax issue was resolved I agreed to help them temporarily until they could find a new pastor. As it turned out we stayed for thirteen months before heading back.

We met a young man named Gulliver Bena, a friend of one of the members, Randy Stype, whose dad had retired from the

U.S. Navy. Gully was a good-looking young man. His father was an American who had abandoned him and his mother in the Philippines and gone back to the States where he lived in Las Vegas, Nevada. Gully entered a national competition called *Mr. Pogi,* meaning Mr. Handsome. He was on TV and finished third in the nation. As well as cash prizes the winner was guaranteed a movie contract, but Gully said the only thing he wanted out of it was to get enough money to go meet his dad.

The Stypes won Gully to the Lord and he started coming to the church and was one of a group of fifteen that we baptized one day at the beach. The church had no baptistry so when we had several candidates ready we would go to the beach for a day and hold a service there. The key to baptizing in the ocean is to catch the waves before they break. Gully was one of the last that day and all the others had gone well, but when I got to Gully a wave broke behind me just as I was putting him down and we didn't get his head under water. So we did it again and when I put him down his one foot stuck up in the air, but I figured we'd got him all wet so it was good enough.

Before we left the Philippines to go back to Kenya Lhey was able to lead Gully's mother to the Lord. Gully had become like a big brother to Jonathan and spent a lot of time at our apartment, and we were all heart broken when he came down with rhabdomyosarcoma, a rare cancer of the muscle tissue. With the Stypes' help he was finally able to get to the States to get treatment in Hawaii, but he wanted to see his dad. Gully was taking chemo and radiation in Honolulu when we came home on furlough. He had not yet seen his dad and when he seemed to show a little improvement a gentleman in the hospital sponsored his trip to Las Vegas where he reconciled with his dad.

My dad and brother, Randall, also lived in Las Vegas and we planned a trip there as soon as we arrived. Gully's mother was worried that Gully would get worse without his treatments, but he told her, "If I don't go I may never see my friends again." We picked up Gully in Las Vegas and met his dad, then started east. He wanted to see the Grand Canyon so we traveled by there, went to Monument Valley, over Wolf Creek pass in southern Colorado, and then to Dodge City on our way to Springfield, Missouri to our home. By this time the Stypes had moved from the Philippines to

Charlotte, North Carolina, so we drove on to Charlotte so Gully could see everyone.

Gully had a shunt and medicine to take daily, but in Charlotte he started feeling very poorly so we got him a flight back out to Hawaii. His mother met him at the airport and they went straight to the hospital. We had brought Rachel with us to the States on a tourist visa. She and Gully had been close so when he started asking for Rachel we flew her out to be with him. She arrived at the hospital just as they were transporting Gully to a hospice facility.

I had a Cincinnati Pops CD of western music including a rendition of Happy Trails to You with Roy Rogers singing. Gully loved the song and we played it over and over on our trip across the States. That night in Hawaii he and Rachel sang it together one more time before he went to sleep. We called the next day, a Sunday, and gave him our last thoughts, but Lhey, Jonathan and I were so broken up we could hardly speak. Gully was so weak he could hardly move and he never opened his eyes, Rachel said, but when he heard our voices he mustered his remaining strength and reached for the phone. After I spoke to him he said, "Thank you, Pastor Lance."

Rachel was sitting with Gully holding his hand as he started to fail. She said to him, "If you see the angels coming, try to raise your hands." He hadn't spoken for hours and then all at once his eyes opened, he sat up in bed, raised his hands to the ceiling and shouted out, "Praise the Lord." His body fell back on the bed and lingered on awhile longer, but Gully had already departed to Glory. He was only twenty-two.

Gully was the kindest, most decent, caring and humble person you would ever hope to know. In his short life he was as godly a man as there could be. One time while praying with Rachel he thanked the Lord for giving the cancer to him and not one of his friends. His last words to his nephew, Nathan, were to read the Bible every day and trust Jesus as his Savior. After he died Rachel was able to lead his sister to the Lord.

I was on my way to a mission conference in Phoenix, Arizona and planned my trip to loop around through Las Vegas to see my dad first. I also wanted to see Gully's dad again. I called him and spent about two hours with him one afternoon sharing the gospel. He gave me every reason in the world why he didn't need the Lord, and I finally prayed in my heart, Lord you'll have to take care of him, I don't know what else to say. Just then he said to me, "Can I accept the Lord now?" Gully's cancer led to his entire family being saved.

We were driving around the Subic Bay Metro Authority, the old U.S. Navy base, which the Philippine government had turned into a Freeport zone. They were selling the old Navy houses to people who were moving into the area so we went around to look at our old house. We saw an *Aeta* on the road near the golf course and as we came around to the hill that hid Pamulaklakin we noticed that the little trail that we had followed had been widened for vehicles so I drove back into the jungle. The village was gone and nobody was there, but there was one little bamboo house in the trees. I thought of Fletcher and Domingo and wondered if they were still around.

The tax issue in Kenya sort of blew over after awhile and one of the missionaries found a loophole that we'd all been looking for and we were able to return to Kenya. By applying for a temporary tax number we had what we needed with no obligation to pay personal income taxes. The government wasn't pushing the issue anymore and no one ever questioned our temporary number.

The college was also liable for medical insurance and social security for our workers if we had four or more full time employees. I had three full time workers and one part time, so we were under the window, and as it was I paid for all their medical expenses anyway.

When we returned to Kenya in 2009 after our second furlough we heard of an opportunity in the Tassia Coffee plantation five miles north of Ruiru town. It had a large chapel big enough to comfortably hold over two hundred people that the owner had built for the permanent workers who lived on the plantation, but it was not being used. There were three housing areas, one in front of the chapel, another two hundred yards away on the other side of the mill area, and another across the road nearly a mile away. Two hundred fifty people lived permanently on the plantation. It was a perfect setting for a church.

I presented the opportunity to our college students. Five were about to graduate, but not one was interested. We decided we couldn't pass it up and started our second church at the plantation. I took Sammy and we met with the manager, Bwana Joseph, who lived in a "mansion" at the top of the hill above the chapel. It was a large house built around 1930 that had been added onto piecemeal over the years. It turned out Joseph was also a Baptist and was happy to have us start a work.

When the coffee beans ripen the workers go into the fields with bags and pick the good beans. They leave their bags by the road and at the end of the day a tractor pulling a trailer picked up the bags and took them to the mill. When the workers arrived they picked up their own bags and took a two-gallon size bucket, separated leaves and twigs, and filled the buckets with beans. These were then poured into a vat on top of a shed. The workers were paid per bucket.

The beans were then washed down a chute to machines that de-shelled them, and the beans were then drained down into vats to be washed. They were separated according to orders and left in the vats until the right caffeination was reached. The longer the beans sat the more the caffeine was diluted. The beans were then put through a big circular drying machine and spread out on tables to dry in the sun.

At the end of the day the manager took us below the vat where the workers were separating their beans and introduced us. He encouraged all the people, mostly ladies but some men, to attend our services. Then I spoke to them and Sammy informed them of the time.

The first Sunday we had fifty-four people including children. Week by week more came until we were averaging around a hundred twenty. Lhey taught the children in a back room, I taught the adults, and we brought one of our Bible college students, Stephen Kiriungi, to teach the teens. Another young man working on the plantation, Lelenguya helped Lhey with the children. Attendance was high when the beans were still growing, but when they ripened and the harvest started our attendance dropped to almost just children.

Lelenguya lived in the third housing area across the road at the far end of the plantation. A stream runs along the border of the property and on the other side is the backside of the Ruiru prison. One Sunday Lelenguya came to church with a swollen black eye and cuts and bruises around his face. His legs were also injured and he walked slowly, stooped over. I asked him what happened and he said that two prisoners had escaped from the prison and apparently ran across the plantation to get away. Guards from the prison came looking for them and when they saw Lelenguya working in the field they accused him of helping them escape. He hadn't even seen the escapees but the guards nearly beat him to death trying to get a confession out of him. Lelenguya remained faithful and was a blessing to the work.

On our first anniversary we had my uncle, Dr. Carl Boonstra, come as our guest speaker. We set an attendance record with 157, and fed them all a meal at the plantation mansion. Joseph's son, Victor, was crippled in a wheelchair and unable to make his way down the dirt trail to the church. On the anniversary day he was in his room eating by himself, and when I visited with him and shared the gospel he asked the Lord into his heart. We saw 124 people accept the Lord at the plantation.

The work went well for a year and a half but then the owner of the plantation sold it for a land development plan. There was more money in the land than in the coffee. They offered to sell us the chapel for fifty thousand dollars, but I didn't have the money, and once the workers moved off there would be no one there until a community developed. To make matters worse, a cult group purchased the entire plantation. They planned to build a cult society for their members. It would never have worked for us to build a church in the middle of their community.

At the same time I resigned from the college. I had been the administrator for eleven years and I felt it was time for new leadership with new ideas. I was also running out of money. Our support in Kenya had grown twenty-five percent over the years, while the cost of living in Kenya had risen three hundred percent and our family had grown by two. In 20009 we adopted Lhey's youngest cousin, Hannah, after her father had died. We were to the point of just surviving. I had no work funds left for any projects. Our Land Rover, which had been a lemon from the beginning, was more often in the shop than not. As we came to the end of our third term on the field we had no obligations left to churches or the college, only Brenda's support, which we handled through an account we set up with Sammy.

Chapter Eight
Changing Fields

When we started for home on furlough in 2011 our plan was still to return to Kenya. Jonathan had two years of school left and we wanted to be back for his senior year of high school at the Rosslyn Academy, a Southern Baptist mission school with a U.S. curriculum in Nairobi. Jonathan had gone to school there most of his life.

A month before we left Kenya Lhey ate something one afternoon and had an allergic reaction to it. Her right eye puffed up and turned red and watery and she could hardly breathe. As soon as we arrived home she took some Benadryl and that seemed to help, but we got in the car and started off for the hospital.

Jonathan's pediatrician had been Dr. Sydney Nesbit at Gertrude's Garden Children's Hospital. He also had children at Rosslyn Academy and I'd see him from time to time. I called him to see if he could see Lhey because his hospital was the closest, but he told me it would be better to see a friend of his at Agha Khan Hospital. Agha Khan was a little farther, but closer than Nairobi Hospital, and we were still stuck in rush hour traffic. The doctor had gone home and came back, but we got to the hospital first and waited.

By the time he arrived Lhey was completely over whatever had stricken her. He examined her and then gave her a steroid shot that he said would help. It didn't. Lhey actually then had a reaction to the steroid and began having problems breathing and swallowing. Then she would wake up in the night unable to breathe and started having panic attacks.

We left Kenya and stayed four weeks in the Philippines but Lhey's condition continued to get worse. We saw several doctors but nobody could diagnose her problem. On our first attempt to fly home she got so sick at the airport we had to see the on call physician and missed our flight. Two weeks passed before she was well enough to try again, but on this occasion it was raining and the trip to the airport took over four hours. Lhey started feeling bad again and when we arrived at the airport she had another panic attack and wanted to go home. I told her the ride home would be another four hours on the same rough road and we might as well get on the plane. She agreed.

McCarran Airport at Las Vegas had just become an international airport and we got a flight there. It stopped over in Vancouver for three hours, which was good for Lhey. She stretched out on a couch and got some rest. When we arrived in Las Vegas my brother picked us up and we went straight to a doctor. He looked down her throat and said it looked inflamed. She had dysphasia, a lump in the throat syndrome that was so bad she actually couldn't swallow even though the passage was clear. The panic attacks continued in the night and we rushed to the hospital several times only to find when she got there she was okay.

We finally got back to Springfield and Lhey asked our family doctor if they could do a sleep study. The doctor scheduled it and within minutes of her falling asleep they knew part of the problem. She had sleep apnea. It was unusual for someone with her body size to have it, but her blood oxygen level during sleep had dropped all the way to 78%. With a CPAP breathing machine she started sleeping through the night but she still had problems including acid reflux and other things nobody could diagnose.

Our original family doctor got impatient with her, mostly I think because he was incompetent to find the answer, but when I saw on her medical record that the doctor had stated he thought she was faking it and I was facilitating her we looked for another doctor. Think it through, I thought. We didn't ask him for any specific diagnosis, neither were we seeking some kind of financial benefit. How would we have profited by playing this game?

We tried everything, even acupuncture and holistic methods, things our insurance didn't cover, but nothing helped. But something was definitely wrong with Lhey. She dropped from 110 pounds to 79, more than a quarter of her body weight. That was no doubt serious.

We had seen twenty-two doctors including two neurologists and a dental surgeon and the one common conclusion was that she was suffering from stress. Lhey rejected that idea. We both did. Living in Kenya was certainly stressful but it was no more stressful then than it had been for the preceding twelve years.

Finally we found a new family physician who was determined to figure it out. On one visit he said that he had been reading and what Lhey had sounded to him like a palatal myoclonus, a condition where the soft palate and neck muscles convulse, where there can be clicking sounds in the ears, and where it becomes impossible to swallow. It was so rare, he said, that he had never seen it, but it sounded exactly like what Lhey was going through.

He had just looked in Lhey's mouth as he was describing it. I was beside him looking also and as he stood up before Lhey closed her mouth her uvula suddenly began to have spasms. I told the doctor it's happening now and he quickly looked again and was amazed. The problem with it was that there is no cure. He said the descriptions say it is a condition that sometimes just gradually goes away.

The first step in Lhey's recovery had been the sleep machine. Her blood oxygen level was normal again and she was no longer having the panic attacks in the middle of the night. There was no immediate cure for the other but just knowing what it was gave her a feeling of justification when so many people had thought she was going crazy.

By this time she had gained a little weight but was still not strong and Jonathan was about to start his senior year of school in Springfield, Missouri. We decided it would be best to stay and let him finish school and then see how Lhey's health was doing before going back to the field. After much prayer we also decided, and the Lord gave us peace about the decision, that being so far from good medical help in Kenya might not be the best situation for her. If the doctors were right and stress was a cause of her condition a less stressful place would be a better option. I went to our Mission Office and applied for a field change to the Philippines.

Chapter Nine
I Shall Return

The epic picture of General Douglas MacArthur departing from the Philippines in 1942 is captured in a larger than life statue on Corregidor Island with his immortal words imprinted on the pedestal, "I shall return."

In August 2013 we returned to the Philippines. We were determined to see how Lhey would do. Her weight was back up to ninety pounds and she still wasn't completely well but she wanted to try. The flight from Los Angeles to Manila took fourteen and a half hours. We arrived at 7:30 p.m. and were met by family and friends. The trip to Olongapo was long and we stopped along the way to eat, although no one was hungry, but mostly so Lhey could rest awhile from the drive. We finally got to bed at 1:30 the next morning.

In the Philippines she slept with the breathing machine exactly twice and never needed it again. Her overall recovery was still very slow, she was constantly tired, but she was improving. The sleep apnea simply stopped. It took two more years but she finally seemed to have recovered from everything except the acid reflux and an occasional throat spasm. It had been as the doctor said; most of the symptoms just slowly faded away.

In the two years since we had been in the Philippines two new malls had gone up in Olongapo, one in the city, and one across the river in the Subic Bay Metro Authority (SBMA), on what was the old U.S. Navy base. They weren't huge in comparison with other malls that have been springing up all over Manila in the last thirty years, but they were large enough that we could get what we needed without having to travel to San Fernando an hour away where then nearest other mall was located.

The SBMA Freeport zone was also growing. Hotels had sprung up all along the waterfront. Foreign investments had built a business park and brought thousands of jobs to the region. A Korean ship repair operation named Hanjin built a huge facility on the northwest side of the bay and thousands of people were buying or renting homes in the old Navy housing areas.

We looked around to see if there was anything available and there were houses on the market, but they were far out of our range to buy or even rent. Most of them were small cracker box outfits that were in disrepair and not suitable for us anyway. Then Lhey found us an apartment in town on the fourth floor of a building on Gordon Avenue close to the malls.

It was the largest apartment for the cheapest price we could find and it needed help. I fought a battle with cockroaches our first night, killing twenty-two of them. These were not little baby things, but like you find in Texas, big. Two to three inches big. We also had rats and ants were all over the place, but we cleaned them all out and stayed in the apartment for two and a half years.

The apartment was convenient, walking distance to our old church and close to transportation. Mass transit in the Philippines can get you right to your door. There are the large Greyhound type buses that run the highways all over the country. In the cities there are Jeepneys that run regular routes to every *barangay*. A *barangay* would be comparable to a precinct or district in the States except that they have a much more organized structure. A *barangay* captain controls his district like a mayor might govern a city.

Jeepneys were designed after World War 2 by taking the front end of the U.S. Army Jeeps, putting a bench seat behind the engine for the driver, and a long covered tail end with bench seats down each side. From there tricycles, small 150cc motorcycles with sidecars, take you direct to your destination. We had no place to park a car so we relied on the local transportation and when we needed to go somewhere we would rent a car for about thirty dollars for twelve hours. It worked for us for a time.

When the Navy left Olongapo in 1992 the bar culture all but died. The economy of the city struggled for years while trying to rebuild a business district and waiting for SBMA to be developed. But the city made a comeback. The shells of many of the old buildings destroyed by Mt. Pinatubo still stood, but slowly they were being torn down and replaced. As the city made its comeback, so did the nightlife. It is nothing today like it was in the Navy days, but a new generation of Filipino young people is out drinking and partying on weekends and prostitution, which is technically illegal, is making a comeback. Something else that is growing is the number of transgenders in the city.

The Philippine government has always had a rather cavalier attitude about prostitution. By law it is illegal so according to the government there are no prostitutes. During the Navy days there were "hospitality girls." A sailor could go into any bar, pay a girl's "bar fine," and she was his for the night. The girls then carried the receipt with them in case they were stopped because the police patrolled the streets arresting hookers working alone. The bars had a monopoly on the business. If the bar fine was paid, the hooker was legitimate. They were all in on the system.

U.S. Navy ships had been returning for port calls occasionally for several years, which were a boon for the bars when they came in, but that all came to an end in October 2014. When the USS Pelilieu dropped anchor in Subic Bay, a Marine lance corporal and three of his Navy shipmates went on liberty into Olongapo City to go bar hopping and look for girls. The Marine was barely twenty, not even old enough to legally consume alcohol in the States, but such laws don't matter in the Philippines and the U.S. Navy has always winked its eye about its personnel drinking and shopping for a good time. After all, it's a time-honored tradition for sailors who've been out to sea.

The Marine was picked up by two transgenders calling themselves Barbi and Jennifer and in the morning Jennifer, whose real name was Jeffrey, was found dead in a hotel room, while Barbi had disappeared. The trial outcome was predictable and although the Marine insisted on his innocence, he was found guilty of homicide because murder charges couldn't be proven. The evidence against him was circumstantial, while evidence suggesting his innocence was ignored. He was sentenced to five to nine years in a notorious Filipino prison, but the U.S. wouldn't turn him over unless he was held at a Philippine Army camp in Manila near the embassy.

We didn't realize when we took the apartment on Gordon Avenue how much the nightlife had returned. On our block were five Internet cafes, several restaurants, thirteen bars, and ten hair salons. We learned our first night in the apartment just how loud the nightlife was. Two bars were right next door to our building with Karaoke speakers out on the sidewalk. A third bar at the end of the block had mini-skirted "waitresses" standing by at the door enticing potential customers in. I began to ask the Lord to close those three bars because they were the loudest and most obnoxious, and in a short time He did. In about four months the two bars next to us were boarded up, and a few months later the bar advertising its hospitality girls also went under.

In the hair salons at least half or more of the hair stylists were gay, and half of those were transgenders. There was a hair salon on the ground floor of our apartment. We saw the transgenders every day. I talked with them and I tried to be kind, but I was never able to hold a conversation passed a few amenities. As soon as I spoke to any of them their eyes would get big, then they would start getting coy and then begin to flirt. It was an impossible situation and as soon as we were able to remodel a home east of the city we moved out.

When we arrived we weren't quite certain what we wanted to do. Our first priority was to see how Lhey's health would be and if she would get well. I had a burden to look for the *Aetas* and try to start a ministry among them but we didn't know how to get to the area where we thought they might be. There was a trail behind Pamulaklakin where we first met them that I suspected went up to the village but it was unfit for a car.

Then we met the sister and her husband of a woman we knew at a Filipino church in Springfield, Missouri. They attended Al Bondad's church and were about to hold a medical clinic for an *Aeta* community about an hour to the north of Olongapo. They invited us to go along and we readily accepted.

We met them in front of the Shoe Mart (SM) mall at 6 a.m. We drove around the bay to Subic Town and had breakfast at Jollibee, the Filipino version of McDonald's. Then we were off up the coast to Cabanggan town, where we turned east and drove through the countryside to the village of Cadmang where there is a little Assemblies of God church. It was an interminably long trip. Our driver would accelerate to about fifty kilometers (thirty miles per hour) take his foot off the gas until we slowed down to about thirty, then accelerate back up again. We were going so slow that the hour-long trip took two hours, but at last we were there. The slow drive really didn't matter because we then had to wait nearly two hours for the medical team. They came from Manila through Angeles on the expressway, which ordinarily would have been a faster trip, but a portion of the road had washed out during the last typhoon and they had to take a long detour.

The team finally arrived and the medical clinic was set up in the church building. It was a small wooden structure with a tin roof and a dirt floor. The pastor, Jerome, was an *Aeta* and worked with a village of people across the river and about 15 kilometers over the mountain from Cadmang. Many of those people walked over to the clinic with sick children. Not all the people that came were *Aetas*. There were some mixed mestizos, and some local Filipinos.

As they worked their way through the clinic line they had to stop at a counseling table. Lhey and I offered to help. There were six other counselors as well. These people all spoke Tagalog, but some no English or little, so I prayed with them but Lhey did the witnessing. By noontime everyone had been through the counseling and we had prayed with thirty-eight people to be saved.

The two oldest that we were able to share the gospel with were sisters aged 75 and 76. While we were talking with them a stray dog came around rubbing our legs. I tried to shoo her away but she came back walking right under one woman's legs and sitting on my feet. I tried to scoot her away but she wouldn't move so I reached down to push her and she bit my hand.

Fortunately she wasn't vicious and didn't break the skin. They had some disinfectant and I put quite a lot on the bite. Later Lhey rubbed on some crushed garlic, a Filipino remedy, and after awhile the redness went away.

We also talked to a 98-year-old woman who was a member of the church there. She was the mother of the village chieftain, and she told us she had been in World War 2. We couldn't tell what she was trying to say she did in the war, but a lot of Negritoes all over the islands were guerrilla fighters against the Japanese.

They finally treated 374 people and fed them all a spaghetti lunch. Then for the workers they had prepared a goat *adobo*. It was excellent. It was a very hot day and humid, but well worth the trouble. We'd had our first opportunity to work with *Aetas*, but the burden on my heart was to try and find Fletcher and the group we had worked with on the base. Events forced that effort to be put on hold for a few months.

The management office for the apartment we were renting
was in a small resort hotel on the beach around the bay in the
barrio town of Baretto. It was right on the highway and not hard
to find. We signed a lease and as we were leaving a man came up
behind me begging.

My first reaction was to shake my head and turn away, but
I noticed he was on crutches and his right eye was crossed. I
turned back and looked at him closer. His left leg was barely
down to his right knee, and the ring and pinky fingers of his right
hand were only about as long as to the first joint. "Is your name
Christopher," I asked. "*Opo,*" he replied. Yes, sir.

One night in 2005 Jonathan and I were on Magsaysay, the
main street in Olongapo, at a photo shop to get some pictures
developed. A kid came up to me begging and I shook my head no
without looking. Then as he turned away I noticed he was on
crutches and I said, "Wait." But he didn't.

Not long after I saw him again begging and I asked him if
he'd like something to eat. He nodded his head yes, so I took him
to Wimpy's, a restaurant and bakery, to their bread counter and
bought him some food to eat. He was small, I didn't figure more
than ten or twelve, and he never spoke any English to me, but
whenever I saw him I got him some food. My Tagalog was rusty
at best and I began praying that I could run into him someday
when someone was with me.

One afternoon Jonathan and I were walking down the
street when he came up to us. We were right by a Jollibee, so I
asked him if he wanted to eat. He said yes. Just then the intern at
the church, Steve Mahusay, was coming from the other direction.
I grabbed him and we all ate together and Steve witnessed to
Christopher in the restaurant and he prayed to be saved.

There was no mistaking this was the same boy, but now he
was grown up, and he was tall, about five foot eight, and he spoke
more English now. I introduced him to Lhey and we went over to
Mr. Donut. They had a chicken restaurant right there so we
bought him a meal and Lhey asked him if he had any work. He
said, "My work is begging." No doubt there was no one who
would give the poor guy a job. He was also married and had a
little girl named Joy.

We bought some donuts, and there were two little kids
there begging as well. I never give kids anything because you turn

them into beggars, but in this case we bought them each a donut. Then before we left I gave Christopher 100 pesos to buy some milk for his baby. He said that's the area he lives in now and he's always begging on the street.

What a blessing it was to see this kid seven years later all grown up. Every time we went over to pay the rent I went out on the street and looked for him, but unfortunately I never saw him again.

Al Bondad asked me to preach for him one Sunday. His church was meeting in one of the theaters at the SM mall early before the mall opened. They had close to two hundred people.

I preached on Daniel 5. Five women on my left talked and laughed throughout. Not just whispered and giggled, but out loud. They were sitting on the front row and Al tried to signal them to be quiet but they didn't pay him any attention. I walked over in their direction, looked straight at them, and spoke directly to them. Another time I stood in front of them and got quiet just looking at them. It made no difference. They went on like I wasn't even there.

It's unbelievable how uncaring or uninterested and disrespectful some people can be. What was the point of their even going to church at all? I had to wonder if there was a demonic spirit trying to disrupt the service. In the end it didn't work. I gave an invitation and three people came forward. I took them out in the hall so we could talk and a woman and two men, Nep, Salvador and Jhun, all in their thirties, prayed with me to accept the Lord as Savior.

Anyone who has been in the ministry long is likely to feel opposition on some days. There have been times when I've been well prepared to preach and just stumbled all over myself and felt oppressed. One Sunday morning in Kenya at Kihunguro I was preaching from Proverbs against sin and I guess I stepped on the devil's toes. The road outside was just dirt and the building was about eight feet from the fence along the road. It was hot and we had all the windows open. Right when I got to a major point a sudden gust of wind came up and blew clouds of dust through the windows and then caught the frames and slammed all the windows shut at once. It took everybody by surprise and I thought somebody must not be too happy. On the other hand the Lord was hopefully looking down smiling.

As it turned out FOFBC was again without a pastor. Some of the members began to campaign for the church to call me. At first I told them no. We had other plans to launch out to the *Aetas*.

The situation was not good, however. The former pastor was scheduling the speakers for the church and the church secretary asked me if I would fill in and they began adding me to the schedule once a month. What was irritating was that these fill in speakers would skip Sunday school and preach the same message at the evening service that they had preached in the morning. The secretary then asked me if I would teach the adult Sunday school every week which I agreed to.

The final straw came when the church hosted a monthly pastors meeting with the Fundamental Baptist group in northern Luzon. I attended the meeting along with the head deacon of the church, James Lee. In the last session of the day the pastors began discussing what they could do to get a pastor for FOFBC. They suggested some names, but their concern was that the church would remain within their fellowship.

When I had heard enough I stood to speak. I told them that this was an independently organized church and that securing a pastor was not the responsibility of the pastor's fellowship. We as a church would call whomever we wanted when we found someone. They reiterated their concern that the church remain within their fellowship. I told them the church had no plans to leave them or join any other fellowship of churches, but that we would make our own decision on a pastor.

James Lee agreed with me. After the meeting I told him that if the church still wanted to call me that I would accept on an interim basis with the understanding that I would help them find a full time pastor. He took it to the Advisory Board and they agreed.

In the next few weeks we had two men candidate but they did not accept, and then as we began to prepare for the church's fortieth anniversary the search for a pastor went on the back burner. We began to make large plans for a reunion of past members, a series of guest speakers to include previous pastors and seminary students, and a Bible conference. It suddenly was the wrong time for me to consider leaving.

Four years later as we prepared for furlough we could no longer put it off and we finally had a serious candidate. We had sponsored five young people out of our church to Bible college including Hannah's oldest brother, James Dequina. Their father, Ernie, had in years past been the song leader of the church. He was a small man with a great smile and full of energy, a great servant of the Lord, but he had passed away from leukemia in 2004.

James was in very many ways just like his dad, full of energy and enthusiasm for the work. He was also in his late twenties so a little more matured than the younger men. He had been around the church for years, the people liked him, and we had full confidence that he would be acceptable to the church as pastor when we left.

On September 23, 2013 we had one of the worst floods to ever hit Olongapo. A typhoon was crossing the southern Philippines. It devastated Leyte and Samar, almost leveling the city of Tacloban. It started raining in Olongapo around 9 p.m. It was steady and heavy, but the wind wasn't bad so we had the windows open in our apartment. Sometime around 3 a.m. the wind picked up and blew the rain in on the bed. I got up and closed the windows as the rain kept getting harder. Then we lost power.

In the morning it was raining so hard we thought the typhoon might have changed direction and was passing over us. The water running down off the hills swelled the river as it flowed into town and in the morning when the tide came in the water had no place to go. It backed up everywhere and flooded the city. Not just the little floods a foot or two deep around certain areas, but a monster flood.

One of the reasons we picked our apartment, besides the size, was that our street, Gordon Avenue, was at a little higher level than the rest of the city and almost never had a flooding problem. This day it flooded. It was about knee deep to a Filipino out on the street, and came up our sidewalk and into the hallway and was eight inches deep at the bottom of our stairs. So we stayed inside. The worst problem we had was three leaks in the ceiling, but none were exceptionally bad.

Around town it was much worse. The water was four feet deep at the church and up to the door of the parsonage at the back of the property. At the *Bajac-Bajac* market near City Hall in the center of town the water was six to eight feet deep, up to the roof of Jeepneys. Hundreds of cars were ruined, covered by the muddy, sewage backed up water. On the other side of town by the cemetery the river was so high it washed some ground out and a two caskets floated away. Several houses too close to the banks of the river collapsed and were washed away. It even flooded the roads on SBMA, which has a better drainage system than the town, and which had never happened before.

Around 10:30 in the morning the rain stopped and the tide started going out and by 2:30 p.m. our street had cleared enough for us to go to the mall and get some groceries. By 3:30 a second round of rain started but it only lasted an hour and didn't cause any more flooding.

At about 5:45 the power came back on and we were back to normal. Around town the streets were a foot deep in mud and traffic was backed up everywhere. Trash was all over the streets and people cleaning out their homes were just throwing out everything they had on their first floors; couches, beds, even some appliances and cabinets. They were scooping mud out of their houses with shovels. Stores along the main roads had as much as they could get out in the air to dry. A hardware store had rubber trashcans all over the front filled with water and the workers were washing off all of their product. At least the tap water was still potable and flowing in the pipes.

Along the roads people had the hoods of their cars open trying to dig the mud out of the engines and doors open trying to scoop the mud out of the floors and seats. We were thinking how glad we were that we decided to get the apartment first rather than a car. I'd hate to think of having a brand new car caught in that flood.

A medical doctor at our church, *Doctora* Cacho said that when the water started rising at her house she put her important things up on her bed. But the water kept coming up until her bed was floating and when it got higher the bed tipped over and all her stuff fell into the water. She retreated upstairs with her housedress on and it was the only clothing she had that didn't get soaked and soiled so she wore it to the prayer meeting at church the next night.

Church members Leo and Esther Edillon who live in Baretto had water up to their waists in their house and spent two days cleaning it out. He said all the furniture was ruined, but it had happened before so they would just continue on. Floods are not uncommon in Olongapo, but this one set a record for the city.

We were invited to a birthday party for a relative of one of the members of the church in the town of Iba two hours up the coast. Lhey and I and our youth pastor, J.P. Quintero, went with the family to the Victory Liner bus station. After coffee we got a bus and arrived around 10:30. The family sent two tricycles over to take us to the house.

Ate (Ah-tee) Susing wanted us to witness to her family, but I lost connection with it somewhere. I thought we were going to be talking with a few of the immediate family. It turned out they were having a full-blown party for the fifth birthday of one of the grandchildren, and family, relatives and friends were coming. There were almost 60 people when they all arrived. So I quickly put together a message from the wedding feast at Cana in John 2.

After a show and a couple of games they divided the clan into groups; the children had a teacher, J.P. took the youth, and Lhey and I took the adults. Some of them were pretty old and didn't speak much English, so I spoke and Lhey translated for me. It was the first time we had ever done that together. After I got through the Romans Road, I let Lhey explain her red, black, and white heart illustration about salvation. Then I finished the points of the message, and Lhey did the invitation. We had fifteen in our group and eight of them prayed to accept the Lord. Over at the youth J.P. said nine of them prayed with him for salvation.

I had preached several funerals in Kenya, but I wasn't quite prepared for the onslaught that we had in the Philippines. In a little over three years I had nineteen funerals. Several of those our church hosted so I wound up preaching more than once. Besides preaching at the wake, there would also be a final preaching moment at the graveside before the burial.

Funerals in the Philippines are a little different. They almost always last at least a week. The casket is usually brought to the home with the body under glass and the spouse or other relatives will sit by the casket continually until the wake is over. Outside the wake becomes a party. Relatives and neighbors gather around, set up tables, and play cards and gamble as if nothing tragic had happened. The family then is obliged to bring out snacks and drinks, and if they are wealthy, food to keep the gambling "mourners" happy.

Our church believers usually planned to have a gospel service each night of the funeral. The difficulty is that many families are a mixture of Baptist and Catholic, or one of the other many cults in the Philippines. Often fewer people are concerned with the service than are concerned with their gambling. Many times I've preached to the family and had to raise my voice to overcome the noise of the revelers. It's hard to fathom how people could be only concerned about playing cards, and not respecting the dead, the family, or the service going on.

At one funeral we were involved in, one of our members asked us to hold a service for a relative. The entire family except our member was Catholic and I noticed a significant contrast the night we had our program. We had several of our church members at the house and we sang hymns and then preached a gospel message to the people sitting around. They had listened politely. When we were done the Catholic Church sent a group over. They stood around the casket, sang something liturgical and then spoke to the body, reminding the person to confess and embrace the blessed virgin. We spoke to the living to give them hope. They spoke to the dead who was beyond any further earthly help.

One family close to our church was very poor with a small house and asked if we could host the wake at the church. Of course we allowed no gambling and the body lay in state for only three days. They asked us to preach each night. We arranged for three speakers including myself on the first night. After the service it was already 10 p.m. and I went on home, but at midnight Lhey called me.

"You have to come back over," she said. She was still at the church and the mourners were still gathered around singing and talking. "There is someone you have to meet," she said.

I got dressed, went back to the church, and Lhey introduced me to an elderly gentleman named Bartholomew Diaz. He was 86, and Lhey had just led him to the Lord. He was telling her his story and she wanted me to hear it. He had been a scout with the American Expeditionary Forces of the Philippines in 1941 when the Japanese invaded. He was in Bataan along what was called the Mariveles Line, the last line of defense on the peninsula.

He and two friends of his were in a trench in the line when a Japanese plane dropped a bomb that was coming right at them. They jumped up and got behind a tree with Bartholomew in the middle. The bomb hit the trench and the shrapnel killed his two friends but he was unhurt. He was then in the Bataan Death March and he told us that a Japanese soldier had struck him across the bridge of his nose with the butt of his rifle. "That's how I got this flat nose," he said and laughed.

The most unusual service I ever conducted came about when an able seaman on a container ship from Myanmar died of insulin shock just as the ship entered Subic Bay. His name was Shwe Mya Saw and he was a diabetic. He ran out of insulin on the voyage, went into shock and had a heart attack just as the ship was putting into port. The family turned out to be Baptist and asked the company if they could arrange a funeral service before they cremated the body to return it to Myanmar. An agent of the shipping line looked on the Internet and found our church website. I readily agreed to help and we scheduled the service for the next day.

At the mortuary there was just Lhey and I, our Bible woman, Perl, from the church, the agent from the shipping line, a videographer and three workers from the funeral parlor. They set up a camera in front of the casket, we sang a couple of hymns, and I preached directly into the camera on The Resurrection and the Life from John 11:25. Then I prayed and gave a final personal message of encouragement to the family. Two months later I received a letter from the family thanking me for honoring their relative. They had shown the video to many of their neighbors. Our ministry in Kenya had really become international and here in the Philippines it had too.

At the graveside you never really knew how people will react. Of course that's probably true everywhere. One of the Catholic traditions is to pass young children over the casket. A man will get on either side and they will pick up and hand the children across one by one. The hope is that the children may catch some of the deceased's spirit.

Often at the gravesite the coffin will be opened to let family members touch the body for the last time. When the lid is finally closed people lose total control and start wailing and throwing themselves on the casket, shouting at the deceased to come back. I've heard people say it's not fair that you've left us behind. It can be very sad.

Yet when true believers, those trusting Christ alone for salvation, are buried there is often a dignity that is not seen among non-believers with no hope. There are quiet tears but an acceptance that the loved one is with the Lord. No wild out of control demonstrations.

An interesting side note: The priests at Catholic funerals in the Philippines never go to the cemetery. I don't know why but have often surmised that it is because they have nothing beyond their rituals to say. Many times I've been asked to say something at the burial to try and comfort the mourners and it's enabled me to have the last word on the hope of salvation in Jesus Christ.

I first came to the Philippines in 1985 and on my first Sunday in the country I went out into town to find a church that had been recommended to me. One of my squadron mates drove me out. The church was right outside the base on Gordon Avenue, but the road was full of potholes and myriad signs from the bars and restaurants jutted out over the sidewalk. Between all the signs and dodging potholes big enough to swallow a small car we both missed the church I was looking for. At the end of the block there was a sign for Fundamental Baptist Church, Services in English, so I decided to attend that one. As it turned out that church would be a part of my life for many years to come.

It was a small church meeting in a garage. I sat on the middle isle about halfway to the front. When the service was over a young woman sitting across the isle from me introduced herself and asked me three questions. "Are you on the base?" "Yes," I replied. "Are you married?" "No," I said. "Are you going to marry a Filipina?"

I thought, good night you are forward. The next person I met was an older woman and she asked me the same three questions. Then I met the pastor and he asked me the same three questions. I had not yet become enchanted with the beauty of the Philippine woman, and as pushy as they seemed it's probably surprising that I ever did. But in the end they knew! And in the end I had gone to the Pearl of the Orient and brought home the pearl.

The next person I met was a jolly, round-bellied man with an ear-to-ear smile and a boisterous voice. He offered to show me all around the town and his house out in the mountain that he called the farm. His name was Jose, but everyone called him Brother Joe. I would have an off and on friendship with him over the years. He was nice to know because he took me around in his little Tamaraw jeep, but the down side was he was always trying to raise money. For himself. When he tried to push his niece off on me it strained the relationship to the max, but somehow we restored our friendship.

In 2013 he was one of the first to push the church to call me as their pastor and he rejoiced when I accepted the position. But he started having kidney problems and his health faded quickly. In January 2014 he was in the hospital and we anointed him with oil and prayed over him. He recovered and went home and when we saw him at his birthday in February he looked like his old ornery self. But very quickly his health went away again and one April morning his adopted daughter looked in on him and found his lifeless body with the same ear to ear smile on his face.

We hosted his funeral and preached five nights before having the final burial service. It was the strangest service I ever saw. Several people, including an adopted son, gave testimonies of their experience with Brother Joe. Every one of them told of some rotten thing he had done and what a flawed character he was before contrasting that with some kindness he had showed them or how through his Bible Basketball ministry they had come to the Lord. It was just strange. Finally his daughter then leaned over the glass above his face and shed so many silent tears that we could hardly tear her away from the casket, but when she was through she sat down and told us she was ready. Then they took the body away to the crematoria. No more pain, only a quiet assurance of a future reunion.

Chapter Ten
Language

One of the first things a missionary has to learn going to a foreign country is a language. Even in today's modern world where most countries learn English as at least a second language, many people still do not know English, particularly the very old and the very young. So becoming proficient in a language becomes vitally important. I learned this lesson by experience long before becoming a missionary.

In late 1991 a carrier battle group had made a port call at Subic Bay. One night we had an exercise with the F-14 Tomcats off the ship. Three of us went out with several F-14s and when our mission was done the F-14s went home first because our little A-4s were more fuel efficient and could stay out longer.

While the fleet was in port the air wing landed at the Cubi Point runway, but the last Tomcat in had a landing gear problem and put his hook down for an arrested landing. When he landed his hook caught the cable, but it somehow wrapped around the unsafe gear and he was stuck. The runway was closed while emergency crews tried to get the plane untangled.

Prior to the Mt. Pinatubo eruption Clark Air Base had been our alternative landing field. It was only thirty miles in a direct line, but Clark was closed. Our only other alternative was Manila's Ninoy Aquino International Airport. It was sixty-five miles away, but there hadn't been a U.S. fighter plane land there since World War 2.

We orbited overhead as long as we could but we finally began to run low on fuel and one-by-one we peeled off for Manila. I was the last to go and called our base to inform them. The C.O. got on the phone to our parent command and they called the U.S. Embassy, and then called me back. "Whatever you do," the Flight Duty Officer said, "don't let them park you at the airline terminals. We don't want to create an international incident." At the time tensions were high between the U.S. and the Philippines over the negotiations over the base lease.

We landed at Manila and the taxi directors there didn't know what to do with us, so they parked us on a taxiway a good distance from the air terminals. We shut down and got out, and the first Filipino crewman I saw I spoke to in Tagalog. I greeted him and told him we needed a start cart, a fuel truck and an elbow sleeve to fit our fuel receptacle.

He was surprised to hear me speaking in Tagalog, but from that moment he became my best friend. He drove me all over the airport looking for the things we needed. We found them at Villamore, the Philippine Air Base connected to the airport, and soon we were refueled and ready to go, and we got out without creating an international incident.

What I learned from that experience, however, was that even a rudimentary knowledge of a language would go a long way to opening doors. When people know you respect them enough to learn their language they often become very friendly and helpful. This would be invaluable for a missionary.

When we went to Kenya I went to language school to learn Swahili, but Lhey studied my books and picked it up on her own. She has a knack for languages. In the Philippines the national language is Tagalog, English is taught as a second language, but everybody comes from one of over four hundred language groups. Lhey is Ilonga and speaks Ilongo. She also knows Cebuano and a little Pampangan. So learning Swahili on her own was not difficult for her.

We found some interesting similarities between Tagalog and Swahili. A lot of words were spelled the same or sounded the same but had different meanings. In the Philippines they have a little round green bean that they call *mungu*. When we arrived in Kenya we found they have the same beans for sale in the local markets.

The first time I saw them I said, "Look, Lhey. They have *mungu* beans." Several of the Kenyans around us gasped and some gave us strange looks. I didn't know what I had said that was so wrong until a few weeks later in language school I learned that *mungu* in Kenya is the word for God. Essentially I had said, "We have God beans." No wonder everybody looked at me so funny.

The word that gave me the most trouble, however, was the little word *ako*. In Tagalog *ako* means "me." In Swahili the root *ako* combined with a prefix "y" (*yako*) means "you." I turned that around and embarrassed myself many times.

English is growing as a second language in many countries around the world. It is the primary language used in international aviation. But even in a culture where many or most people speak English it is often difficult to communicate exactly what you are trying to say. Sometimes people pronounce words in English differently leading to misunderstandings.

One day several of the pilots at my squadron in the Philippines went up to the Cubi Officer's Club for lunch. When we finished our meal one fellow and I decided we'd like to have some pecan pie for dessert. We asked the waiter.

"No," he said. "There is no pecan pie."

"What kind do you have?"

"There is a chocolate cream, coconut cream, apple, peach and 'peck-in' pie," he said putting the emphasis on the first syllable.

We decided to try the "peck-in" pie and then asked if we could get it alamode. "Yes, sir," he said. "And can you heat the pie?" I asked him. "Sure," he replied.

A few moments later he brought us our pies. He had heated them in an oven and the little pie plates were so hot he carried them on a large dinner plate, and the ice cream was melted all over the pie.

But he had given us exactly what we had asked for: pie, ice cream, heat. He understood what we were saying, but somehow we had not communicated. This becomes a particularly delicate issue when it comes to ministry and preaching the gospel. You can't afford to have people misunderstand the message of salvation or the method of receiving it by faith in Christ alone.

Chapter Eleven
The End of the Search

When we returned to the Philippines our first goal was to see if Lhey would get well and slowly she began to improve. FOFBC wanted to call me, but I didn't want to commit myself to the church full time because deep in my heart I wanted to try and find Fletcher and see if we could have a ministry to the *Aetas*. I knew about where the village was in the mountains but I didn't know how to get there.

One day I was talking with Matt Quinoveba, a former deacon at our church, and he said he knew how to get to the place. The village was called Pastolan. Matt had worked for the Navy in the '80s and '90s, and when they were going to have a reduction of workers Matt was about to lose his job. So I wrote a letter of recommendation for him and the supervisor at his workplace decided to keep him. Matt was always happy to help me with anything. He offered to go with James and me to help us find the village.

Matt knew the way, and it wasn't hard to find once we were there. It was March 24, 2014 when we took the zigzag highway to the little town of Tipo and got a tricycle to take us up to the village. The road was paved, but not in very good condition. It took us to a gate at the foot of Mt. Santa Rita, where a tower and TACAN station were located. It was a primary navigational point back in the Navy days, but civilian aircraft don't use the TACAN, and the station today is unused. The road up the mountain is blocked off. The fence marked the boundary of the SBMA reservation and guards were at the gate monitoring who came in.

From the gate the road went up to a high ridge and was so steep that the driver asked me to lean forward so my weight wouldn't cause us to tip over backwards. Then he drove up zigzagging left and right to keep up enough momentum to get over the hill. With my weight added to three others the bike barely had enough horsepower to get to the top. And then there was a second equally steep hill.

The backside was a little gentler going down and a smoother ride but it got steep again at the bottom. There we came to a river with a wooden bridge in such great disrepair we wondered if we could cross. No problem. Big vehicles used it all the time, but it sure was rickety. The rails on the side were falling over and the 2x12 planks making the roadbed were rotting, splitting, and coming loose. A triple layer of the planks had been laid down originally but several of the top layer were loose and half of them were missing.

The village had one main road going up the next hill to a Y intersection about two-thirds of the way to the top. The government had just paved the road with concrete the previous January to a point a little passed the intersection. Small bamboo and wood houses, some with grass roofs and some with tin, and some cinder block houses lined the road. Most were in poor condition or unfinished. An electric line had also just been run to the village the year before and most of the buildings along the road had electricity, but those built farther off the road in the jungle did not.

The tricycle driver took us to the chieftain's house about halfway up the hill. It was the nicest structure in the village; a cinderblock building with plastered walls, glass windows, and a nice tiled roof. The chieftain wasn't in, but we met two of the tribal council members. They were brothers, Angelito Delcosar, who goes by Lito, and Manuelito, who goes by Manuel. We told them we were interested in starting a church work in the village and Lito showed us around.

We learned that there was an Assembly of God church in the village that only meets on Sunday mornings, and the Catholics use the *barangay* hall on Saturday afternoons occasionally to hold a mass. Two years prior the government had built an elementary school, K-6, and provided a very nice stretch jeepney that carries 24 people at a time, which they use to take their older kids to special classes for them at Jackson High School in Olongapo.

We went to the school and talked with two of the teachers, but the principal wasn't there. School was out for the summer break. They told us that they had no one to teach the religious education classes and gave us the cell number of the principal so that we could contact her about teaching.

From there we walked on up the road to the basketball court at the *barangay* hall and met two more of the tribal council members, one a woman named Des. Finally I got to ask the question that was haunting my mind. "Does Fletcher Abraham or Domingo live here in the village?"

"Domingo died many years ago," Des said. "But Fletcher's home is over there." She pointed up the road to the other side and we walked up to the place. Fletcher's house was back off the road behind two large trees. It was only about fifteen feet square made of unpainted cinderblock walls with shutters over glassless windows, and a tin roof.

Fletcher had a very large family. We met his brothers, cousins, in-laws and grandchildren. Des, it turned out, was also a cousin of Fletcher, and her husband, Pablo, worked as a forest ranger. He was at the gate at the base of Mt. Santa Rita when we came in.

Bonifacio, called "Boni," lived next door to Fletcher. He was very anxious to show me a certificate he had received from the U.S. Marines. He used to be a guide for the Bravo Company patrols that went around the base perimeter back in the Navy days. He was very proud of his certificate.

"Fletcher works at Pamulaklakin," we were told. I asked if that was near the old village where we first met Fletcher in 1992. "Yes," she said. Now it was a resort area for tourists. The last time we had been there seven years ago we saw one bamboo building with no people around. Now I had been so intent on finding our way to Pastolan that I hadn't even thought of looking there again.

"He'll be back at five o'clock," Des said.

We went on up the hill to the end of the paved road, and then on up the dirt road to the top of the mountain. On the way we passed three houses on the left that formed a little triangle and stopped to talk with a man named Sonny. Sonny was also on the tribal council. In talking with Sonny we discovered that he was one of the kids that was in our little Sunday school to at Pamulaklakin in 1992. He remembered the Americans coming to their little village. On our next visit we met his older sister, Marilyn, who vaguely remembered us, but remembered well the Sunday school and that an American and his Filipina wife who came to teach them.

I was growing anxious about meeting Fletcher. We were about to walk on up to the end of the village when a tricycle came over the top of the hill and down the road. As it passed Sonny shouted, "There's Fletcher!" He hollered for them to stop and called for Fletcher.

The tricycle slid to a dusty stop and a little man wearing a ball cap, tank top, shorts and flip-flops sitting between two others in the open side car got out. There was no mistaking him. This was the same man who was the chairman at the Pamulaklakin village in 1992. I had fairly forgotten how small Fletcher was. When we last saw him he had his head shaved and he was pretty solid, but he was barely five feet tall. Now his head was no longer shaved, his hair was white, and he was very thin, but I recognized him at first glance. I towered over him until I stepped down slope beside him.

"*Naalala mo ako?*" I asked him. Do you remember me?

He nodded his head. "Yes," he said, and stuck out his hand to shake mine, and he gave me a hug. Then he pointed his finger at me and said, "You were at Pamulaklakin."

His English had improved considerably, and my Tagalog a little, but we were able to understand each other and had a pleasant conversation like two old friends. We walked back down the road to his house and he showed us around. The house is on the edge of a slope, and in the back it had a room made of bamboo walls with a dirt floor that served as a kitchen. There were no stairs and it was about a two-foot step up to get into the main house, but there was a concrete floor inside.

By this time, however, it was near sunset and we needed to get off the mountain before it got dark and no more tricycles were running.

"*Babalik kami,*" I told Fletcher. We shall return! "I'm not sure how soon because we have other things going on, but we want to try and start a church work here in the village."

"*Ayos.* It's good," he said. "We need something here."

I was a little surprised by the comment considering his attitude years before, but I went home rejoicing. I had found Fletcher.

Chapter Twelve
A New Ministry Begins

Two months passed before we were able to make it back but Matt and James came along and Lhey and Ethan joined us. We arrived about 3 p.m. and Des took us around the village. First we went to the bottom of the village and crossed a tributary creek to the river and looked at a two-acre plot that the *Aetas* had cleared for a campsite. She said several outside groups had used it. There were cashew trees all around but the nuts had been picked. The cashew fruits had been left hanging so we tried them. The fruit is yellow, cylindrical in shape, very juicy and sweet, but the aftertaste dries out your mouth like a sour lemon.

Then we met more people back on the road including a 90-year-old woman named Epang. We wanted to do everything in the proper manner so as not to offend anyone, so we arranged to meet with the chieftain, Condrado Frenillon, the following Friday to explain to him our intentions.

Next we walked back up to the top of the village and looked at potential locations to build a church building. We were there when Fletcher came over the hill behind the driver on a motorcycle. I called him when he went by and he stopped and met Lhey and Ethan, then walked us back down the hill to his house.

Next door to Fletcher's house we met an elderly man named Mario sitting in a chair with a piece of plastic bag wrapped around his arm. He had an open wound and that was the only bandage he had. Fortunately Lhey had ointment and Band-Aids in her purse. Talk about prepared. Once she put the Band-Aid on, Fletcher decided he wanted one for a scratch on his leg too.

Mario's house was next to the road. It was small, about eight feet wide and eighteen feet long with three small rooms. At the near corner Mario's wife, Violeta, operated a little store and sold items through the window. The door opened into the middle room which had a cot and a few cooking utensils, and at the far end was a homemade double size bed made of 2x4s and bamboo with a blanket but no mattress or pillows.

There was an open space under the trees in front of Fletcher's house and I asked him if we could hold a Bible study there. He said that was good and we could meet any day at 5 p.m. While I talked with him Lhey talked with the ladies that were around and they decided to have a picnic the next weekend at Pamulaklakin.

Friday morning came with clear skies so we got a car and Lhey and I, along with Matt Quinoveba, J.P. Quintero, and James Dequina from our church, drove onto SBMA to meet the chieftain, Condrado Frenillon. Des had told us he worked at the *El Kabayo* horse stables so we went there first and met his grandson who told us Condrado worked at a canteen by the main road. We drove back and found the canteen, but the chieftain had left. A worker there had his cell number so we called him and he said he would be back at 3 p.m.

We went on over to the resort at Pamulaklakin. In 1992 Fletcher had been the "chairman" of the small group of fifty that lived there. When the U.S. Navy base closed at the end of 1992 and the Subic Bay Metro Authority took over, they forced the people to move back up into the mountains to the main village at Pastolan.

When we saw it in 2005 it was still undeveloped. Now it was a tourist site that an American company had built for the *Aetas* only two years before. They sold hand carved trinkets, gave nature tours in the forest, and provided demonstrations on *Aeta* culture, making a fire using just bamboo, cooking meals in sections of bamboo and making eating utensils out of the bamboo.

The trail to Pastolan had been widened to accommodate motorcycles and tricycles, but it was still very rough and rocky, and not suitable for cars. The people rode if they could afford the twenty-five peso fee, or walked the three kilometer distance to and from Pastolan.

At the spot where we originally parked the car to hike back into the village the trees had been cleared to make a driveway and parking area wide enough for several cars. A cinderblock house had been built on a hill back in the trees behind the parking area to be used for an office and storage. Beside the drive a row of kiosks were set up where the *Aetas* sell trinkets and wild honey.

They had a water pump and an outhouse, and behind the kiosks a concrete staircase ran down the hill to an iron footbridge across the river that led to a nature trail through the jungle and a campsite that can be rented by individuals or groups overnight or for several days. Across the drive next to the main road on the hill where we waved goodbye to the children in 1992 were two covered pavilions with picnic tables.

We met Fletcher, his son Joel, who had a motorcycle and works as a deliveryman, Lourdes, and some others. After showing us around we went up to one of the pavilions on the ridge. A man named Samson cooked our rice *Aeta* style. He cut a section out of a bamboo pole, very adeptly cut a lid into it, filled it with rice and water, replaced the lid, and then boiled it over an open fire. We had brought two chickens and some *pancit* (noodles) and water. When the rice was done about ten of the *Aetas* joined us to eat. Samson then very carefully split the rice cooker in two to reveal the rice. Then he split other bamboo sections for plates, and made cups for us to drink our water.

The rice from the bamboo was drier, but had a wild, smoked taste to it, while the rice from our rice cookers was much more moist. Funny thing was we all wanted to experience the bamboo rice, which I found to be quite tasty, but the *Aetas* all wanted the rice from our cookers.

I asked Fletcher about *Aeta* customs and beliefs. The *Aetas* have no written history and what they know seems to go back only as far as their own memories. Fletcher told me of his parents but had no knowledge of his grandparents. In World War 2, he said, the *Aetas* hid in the jungles. They only had bows and arrows and were afraid of the Japanese. If they found a lone soldier in the forest they would attack him. Otherwise they tried to avoid them.

There is an *Aeta* legend about an ancient chief called *Apo Butak*, who went hunting in an area on SBMA near the Cubi Point airfield known as *Boton*, and was never heard from again. *Apo* means the head, or the chief, and *Butak* means hunchback. This hunchback leader got lost around the same time as Holy Week. Every year during the week before Easter nearly the entire village makes a pilgrimage to *Boton* as a memorial. They go there, camp out all week and fish in the river and the bay. It's about five miles over the hills from the village. I asked if they were still searching for *Apo Butak* and they all laughed.

In 2015 we had to cancel our Bible study on Easter weekend because nobody was around in Pastolan. The next year, however, they invited us to visit their campsite in *Boton* and we had a lunch of rice and fresh fish. With that invitation, more than anything else that had happened, we felt like the people had accepted us into their community. We were no longer outsiders.

Fletcher had a large family. He had eight children of his own, six boys and two girls, and it seemed like half the people on the upper end of the village were either his siblings or cousins. His youngest child, Elvin, was born in 1996, but it had been a difficult labor and his mother died in childbirth.

The *Aeta* language is called *Ambala* and we had our first lesson in the language. *Hita lagyu mo?* What is your name? *Ambala* is a dying language. Only the old people speak it regularly. Everyone else knows Tagalog and in the school the children are taught English as a second language. Many outsiders who have moved into the village also speak English to some degree.

The people of this village, although they are very superstitious, are not animist. They don't worship nature gods like other indigenous tribes, including the *Aetas* around Mt. Pinatubo, do, because being in close proximity to the base they had been under the influence of Christianity. The Assembly of God church, although small, had been there for many years and the *katutubo* (citizens, as they like to be called) considered themselves to be Christians or nothing, but the only God they are aware of is the Christian God. Religion was still superficial to most of them. Not one person that we met in the village had any assurance of salvation. I asked Fletcher if he still wanted to have the Bible study and he said yes.

After the picnic we called Condrado and found he had already returned to the canteen at 1:30, so we drove over to meet him. He was a little bigger and taller than most of the *Aetas*, so I thought maybe that's how he got to be the chieftain! We had a very nice visit with him and he seemed to be real positive about our desires to minister to the village and agreed to meet with the tribal council and us the next Friday morning at eight. Anything we would do at the village as far as a permanent type of ministry, and especially being granted a property on which to put up a building would have to be approved by them.

We were told that the teachers at the elementary school in Pastolan were still at the school so after leaving Condrado we hurried out to the village to try and meet with them, but we arrived at 3:15, and they had just left at 3 p.m. From there we went up to the top of the village to scout out potential locations to put up a church building.

At 5 p.m. we were still at the top of the hill when Fletcher came home on the back of a motorcycle. We told him we'd meet him at his place. We had invited several others to come, but nobody did, so when we got back to his house it was just Fletcher's family and relatives. There were twelve total, three men and nine women, some with small children. We had our Bible study with them. I started with a very basic lesson on the Bible being God's Word, the creation, fall of man, and God's plan for Christ to pay for our redemption, leading into the Roman's Road.

Most of them spoke very limited English, and I didn't speak Tagalog well enough to teach in it, so J.P. translated the lesson for me as I spoke. Then when we got to the invitation I let James handle it so we wouldn't have the delay with the translating. In the end nine of the adults, including Fletcher, prayed with us to be saved! I had been praying for Fletcher for twenty-two years.

Chapter Thirteen
Medical Missions

When we were done with the Bible study Lhey went next door to check on Mario, who had the open sores on his elbow the week before. We brought some peroxide, ointment and bandages. Mario's one wound was healing, but he had a series of sores around his elbow so Lhey treated those, then she witnessed to him, and he prayed with her also to be saved.

Next, he told her about his wife, Violeta. She was inside the store at the window and very ill. She'd had something like dysentery for a couple of weeks and looked emaciated. It was already late in the day, but Lhey talked with her. Then we went back to town and got some medicine.

The next morning we drove up to Pastolan. Violeta was looking real bad, so we offered to take her to the hospital. We took her and her daughter, Irene, to a hospital in town close by our apartment. The doctor wanted to admit her but she refused. She also refused to let them take blood, so all he could really do was give her some medicine and recommend food supplements and what not to eat. So we got the medicine and took her back home. She was very grateful.

When Lhey was getting the medicine Ethan and I waited with Violeta in the car. She asked me if I spoke Tagalog and I said a little, but that Ethan speaks it fluently. So she started talking about our visit on Friday and went on and on, and I just listened picking up little bits and pieces and smiling at her. She's 60 years old, but looks like she could be in her 80s.

The next Friday we had our meeting with the tribal council at the chieftain's house. The council consisted of the chieftain, three other men and two women. Matt and James went along with Lhey and I, and we brought a box of Dunkin Donuts to help break the ice.

We arrived at the chieftain's house at 8 a.m. He was in town and came about five minutes later. We met at a table outside under some trees. I introduced us all and then when I had used up all my Tagalog I deferred to Matt who acted as our spokesman. He explained to them our desire to work in the village holding Bible studies and helping in the school.

Some of the council members were concerned about what

kind of relationship we would have with the Assembly of God church. They have a small church, but the pastor usually only came out on Saturday nights and stayed over for morning services on Sunday. The councilwomen were worried that we would try to steal members from the church and create a conflict.

I told them our history with Fletcher and our desire to minister in the village to the people, but that we weren't interested in religious wars. We wanted to help with the religious education class in the elementary school, have home Bible studies, and help the village in any other way we could with medical clinics and feeding programs if there was a need. They seemed to be happy with that.

The two councilwomen, Marisa and Nina, went with us to the elementary school and we met the principal, Hilda Sisson. She lived in Hermosa, twenty miles away, and rode a bus and a tricycle in everyday for school. All of the teachers were from outside the *Aeta* village. She was overjoyed that we would be willing to help since no one comes to teach the religious education.

She spoke to us for an hour about the village. There was something over two thousand people in the area, but an exact count was unknown. A lot of outsiders drift in and out; some men taking up with *Aeta* women for a while and then leaving. There were 290 children enrolled in the elementary school the last year with 240 being *kulot* (curly hair) and fifty being *unat* (straight hair). The straight hair was the result of intermarrying with outsiders.

Fletcher would later tell me that prior to 1954 there were no *unat* in the village. The *Aeta* didn't like outsiders and outsiders didn't like the *Aeta.* Then one day some workers came into the village and stayed awhile on whatever the job was and they found the *Aeta* women were also beautiful and some took wives. In time some of the *Aeta* men then found that *unat* women were also beautiful and they started intermarrying. (They just moved in together. No one in the village had been formally married.)

School started the next day but the first week was an orientation week so Hilda asked if we could come the following week to start the religious education. I said yes, but asked if we needed to wait for the vote of the town meeting before we started coming. Nina said to me, "Don't worry, just come."

Next Marisa took us to the Assembly of God church.
Pastor Cervantes just happened to be there that Friday which was
unusual. So we met and talked. He had the same concern that we
would be fighting each other. I said no, our interest was to help
the people. We'd be involved in the school, Bible studies, children
programs and maybe Bible basketball programs, but we wouldn't
interfere with his church work or try to steal his members. That
put him at ease, and I figured it would be a big help to us if he
were not opposed to our working there.

Then we made a follow up visit to Violeta. She was a
hundred percent better; color was back in her face, and she was
walking around. Mario, however, suffered from high blood
pressure and had to take tablets for it. He was 78 years old and
walking with a cane, and to get a tricycle to the highway and then
a jeepney to a clinic several miles away to get the medicine was
very difficult for him, so we offered to go pick up the medicine
for him. We had to go all the way back to Olongapo, but then
after lunch we went back up at around 4 p.m. When we arrived
they had a stalk of bananas for us, plus two bags of oysters and a
live crab.

Then a woman named Rosa, who had prayed with us the
week before at our first Bible study, asked Lhey to go with her to
her house so she could give her a bag of mangoes. When they
came back Lhey wanted me to go with them back to the house
and pray over their fourteen-year-old son. He was very sick.

The house was made of bamboo with a grass roof and was
back across a little valley and in the jungle, about two hundred
yards from the road. We passed by five other bamboo houses
along the way with power, but Rosa's house was beyond the
power line. The boy, Erwin, was in a hammock, running a high
fever, coughing and congested. He looked to be quite
malnourished. He was so small we thought he might have only
been nine or ten years old. So we prayed and told them we would
try to get some medicine.

We had to forego the Bible study because by then it was
already 6 p.m. and we had to go all the way back to Olongapo
again for the medicine. Lhey also got them some toothpaste and
toothbrushes plus Listerine to gargle, and we got cough syrup and
Tylenol, and chewable vitamins. It was a quarter to eight when we
started back for Pastolan. I was concerned because the road is

barely more than one lane wide winding through the jungle and by that time it was already dark, the kind of situation we always tried to avoid in Kenya. We went ahead anyway and it wasn't as bad as I had worried. The power line to the village goes right up the road and every now and then there was a light pole, and the only traffic was tricycles, so we got there with no problem.

A niece took Lhey, James and Ethan back to the house while I turned the car around. I had to drive up the hill and find a place level with the road so I could get off the road to turn around. When I walked back into the woods I took a wrong turn in the dark, but Fletcher was right behind me. I didn't realize he had followed me, so he called me and led me up to the house. We didn't have a flashlight, but the niece had a cell phone with a light, so we used that to read the instructions on the medicine. Rosa was grateful to tears. She held my hand with both hands and cried, and then she hugged Lhey and cried more. They couldn't believe we had gone back in the dark with the medicine.

I believe it was at that point when we were willing to come back after dark that many people in the village realized we were serious about helping them. How skeptical they were about us at first was made clear two years later when Irene said, "Many people come to Pastolan. You're the only ones who stayed."

The next week while visiting in the village we met a woman who had just given birth five days before to a son she named Denmark. Denmark was born with a severe cleft palate. Lhey and I discussed helping the baby and I sent out an email to everyone on my mailing list asking prayer for Denmark. One of our friends, Barb Kaiser, wrote back and told us about an organization called Smile Train that took care of cleft palates for free for people who had no means.

I looked up Smile Train on the Internet and found they had an office in Manila so I called. They had three hospitals that they worked out of in Northern Luzon including one in San Fernando, about an hour away from us. When the word got out that we were trying to help Denmark, another woman, Miriam, came to us with her two children, Desiree and Denmar, both of whom had cleft palates. We set a date and took them all to San Fernando.

It was a five day process: first a check in physical, the next day surgery and then two days observation and released on the fifth morning. Smile Train provided the surgery free, but we had to pay for the rooms, meals and medicine and a parent had to stay with the children. Unfortunately for Denmark, Smile Train required the children to be a minimum three months old before they would do the surgery so he had to wait, but we were finally able to get his surgery done about eleven months later.

We had to take Desiree and Denmar back to San Fernando a week later for a follow up visit to remove their bandages. After they had recovered and were eating properly again Miriam began to bring them every week to our Bible studies and after several visits she accepted the Lord.

One day when we were visiting Pamulaklakin we noticed Fletcher wasn't there. He was the overseer of the resort and was almost always there. One of the ladies at the kiosk told me he could barely see and was just wandering around at Pastolan afraid to make the journey down off the mountain.

The next time I saw Fletcher I asked him about it and he said yes, his eyes were bad. He was having headaches, so we took him to an eye doctor who attends our church and Doc Marvin discovered he had cataracts. Cataracts seemed to be a common problem with many of the *Aetas*. It comes from being constantly in the near equatorial sun without sunglasses. The cataracts were strange in that they weren't a gray film covering the entire eye, but a small green colored ring around the pupils

I then asked our head deacon at the church, James Lee, who was a businessman in town and president of the Lion's Club that year, if he knew where we could get cataract surgery done. It just so happened that the Lion's Club was sponsoring a free cataract clinic for indigent people in October, a month later. They had to have the eye medicine in order for the surgery to be done, but the surgery itself was free. I told Fletcher that we would buy the medicine and he agreed to go to the clinic.

On the appointed day I was on my way up the mountain before daybreak so we could get to the hospital and beat the crowd. When we arrived back in town there was already a line of people, but because Fletcher was *Aeta* he was moved toward the front and was twelfth in line.

A medical team with doctors from around the country and some from the States had come to hold the clinic. After his initial consultation he was told to come back the next morning for the surgery, so the following day we were up early to make the trip up to the mountain again. Elvin came with Fletcher this time to help him after the surgery.

At the hospital the doctor explained to Fletcher how the procedure would take place and suddenly he got worried. He didn't quite understand what they were going to do and he decided not to go through with it. He was afraid of losing his eyesight altogether. They called me in and I spoke with him and assured him that they were going to help. He was still hesitant so I suggested they do just one eye first and they could do the other eye when they returned four months later for another clinic. He agreed.

Elvin still didn't understand. When Fletcher went into the surgery he was sitting in the waiting area crying. When Lhey asked him what was wrong he asked, "Are they going to remove his eye?" Suddenly it made sense. They didn't understand that the surgery was just to remove the cataract film over the eye, not the entire eye itself. We assured him that he would not lose his eye, but that he would be able to see again when it was done, and Elvin was greatly relieved.

After the surgery Fletcher had a patch over his eye and had to move very carefully so as not to have any sudden movements that might affect his eye. We drove them back to Pastolan and carefully helped him into his house where he laid down on his bed. Lhey read the instructions on his medicine and explained what he needed to do for the next couple of days. Then we would be back to take him for a follow up visit to check the progress of his eye.

With the patch on his eye Fletcher became somewhat of a celebrity. All the neighbors came around to see what he looked like and ask how the surgery had gone. Three days later I was back to take him and Elvin to the hospital. When they took his patch off he could see so well that he blurted out, "Oh, can we do the other one now?" Unfortunately he would have to wait.

It was noontime when we made our way back to the village so I stopped at a New York Style pizza place and we each had a giant slice of pizza. It was the first time they had ever eaten a pizza. "*Gusto mo?*" I asked Fletcher. Do you like it? "Sure," he said. "*Masarap.*" Delicious.

After the success of Fletcher's surgery others began to approach me about having the surgery done. The next clinic was going to be in February so I started taking names. One of those was a man in his late twenties named Prudencio. He was young, strong, and *guapo* (handsome), and he was totally blind. When he lost his sight his wife left him because he could no longer work. He was so blind that I was afraid it might be too late for him. Another, a woman named Perly, was wearing a New York Yankee ball cap when she passed me on the road, pointed to her eyes and said, *"Catarata."*

When February arrived I brought nine people down to the clinic along with Fletcher to have his other eye done. Prudencio's surgery was a success as was Perly's. Her eyesight had been so dim that she had barely been able to see anything for nearly three years. For those who had both eyes done they put a patch over one eye only and recommended sunglasses for the other eye so that they would be able to get around.

Perly came out of the surgery with one eye covered and the first person to meet her was her husband, George. She pointed at him and said, "It's you! You're getting old." George only needed one eye done, so he let Perly go first so he could help her about until she was fully recovered, and then he planned to have his eye done at the next clinic in October.

We were eventually able to help eighteen people get cataract surgeries including an eighty-year-old woman named Nieves, who lived near the lower end of the village and walked up the hill to our Bible studies. All of them started attending and most of them accepted the Lord. Prudencio became one of our most faithful members.

When we took them back for their follow up visits and to remove the eye patches Perly told the doctor, "You have given me a new life." Shortly after at one of the Bible studies she received the Lord and a new spiritual life as well.

When the U.S. Navy base was open the Navy employed many of the *Aetas* doing various small jobs and some of the men were guides for the Marine patrols. The *Aeta* received paychecks and a bag of rice on time every month from the Navy. When the Navy left the Philippine government made them wards of the state, but for years largely ignored them except for a welfare check every month.

Delivery of the checks was unreliable and when, as during the rainy season, they had few or no visitors at Pamulaklakin, they didn't get paid at all. When we first started the Bible studies the people hadn't been paid in several weeks and many were going hungry. We realized right away that some kind of feeding program might not only be necessary, but be an opening for sharing the gospel with the people as well.

About a year before we arrived the government had run an electric line into the village and many of the houses along the road were hooked up. Those farther away were not. Fletcher very proudly told me, "We are civilized now. We have electricity." He also said the people didn't like to be called *Aeta* anymore. They preferred to call themselves the *katutubo,* which means citizen.

More important for our purposes, in January 2014 the government paved the road from the bridge at the bottom of the village up to the Y-intersection and a little farther just in time for us to begin our ministry in the village. When the rains came and turned the dirt road to mud not even the tricycles would go farther than the bridge at the river. Now we could drive up nearly to the upper end anytime. Coincidence? Or was God preparing the way?

The people had no source of water in their homes, no wells or pipes, no showers, outhouses or even latrines. When they had to use the facilities they just went out into the jungle. So the government also built a large water tank at the upper end of the village and a pipe ran down along the road with taps at various locations. When the tank was full and a valve opened people were able to fill water containers at the taps. It wasn't filtered well and it wasn't enough for bathing, but it became was their running water.

To bathe many of the people would go down to the river at the low end of the village, but it was small and often muddy. The river at Pamulaklakin was a bigger and cleaner watercourse and many of those who lived at the upper end of the village would make the walk three kilometers down the mountain to bathe. But then they had to walk back up the dusty road to the village, which largely defeated the purpose.

The *Aeta* are literally dirt poor and the living conditions were obviously not conducive to good health, especially for the children. Erwin continued to struggle with his health mostly due to malnutrition. Early in 2016 he had become listless and was so emaciated that we took him to the James Gordon government hospital in Olongapo. He was given an IV and admitted into a ward.

The wards in the hospital had twenty beds, no privacy screens, no air conditioning or fans, and were extremely hot and uncomfortable. All the patients shared one small restroom ("CR" or comfort room) in the middle of the ward. No meals were provided so family had to bring food, or if they had come from a distance, family members would often stay in the ward with the patient. The wards were so crowded that people often had to share beds. When Erwin was admitted he was to share a certain bed with two others, but when he, Rosa, and his sister came in, they were so dirty that the other two on the bed quickly arranged to share with other people. So Rosa and her children had their own bed.

When it came time for Erwin to use the CR he insisted on going outside. The hospital wouldn't allow that and as well he had an IV in his arm so it was not possible. He decided at first to hold it in, but when it became impossible to wait any longer he went into the CR, but he had never seen a toilet before and instead of using the toilet he did his business in a corner of the room.

After the orderlies cleaned up the room they gave Erwin a lesson on how to use the toilet. Toilet seats are actually a more recent commodity in mostly more modern buildings and facilities. In most of the Philippines where people do happen to have porcelain toilets they still don't have toilet seats. The hospital didn't either. The next time Erwin used the toilet he sat on the rim of the bowl facing the tank.

It's not hard to understand with the unsanitary living conditions why children especially were constantly plagued by skin and scalp diseases. Psoriasis, dermatitis, ringworm, bleeding or oozing sores, as well as lice were common. One day while I was in the village Fletcher introduced me to his three-year-old grandson, Raymond. Raymond had sores all over his body from feet to scalp.

Lhey had taken pre-nursing at Arapahoe Junior College in Denver before becoming pregnant with Jonathan. Even without finishing the nursing course she knew medicines and treatments well for all kinds of conditions. When I told her about Raymond she got peroxide, antibiotic ointments, gauze and other bandages, soft soaps and towels for cleaning, and off we went to Pastolan.

She showed Raymond's mother how to clean the sores, washing them out with peroxide and then using ointment and covering them with bandages. She helped to shave his head so she could treat the oozing sores on his scalp. When we returned a week later the sores were already scabbed over and Raymond was well on his way to recovery. It then became routine for us to have medicine with us, as Lhey became the traveling nurse making house calls and treating every kid that was brought to her. I began to call it Lhey's Traveling Clinic.

Treating adults was usually a bigger challenge because their wounds were often deep from some work related injuries. The first time I had visited Pastolan a woman passed by smoking a cigarette, which I thought was so unusual that I tried to get her picture. When I raised the camera she turned to face me, but very adeptly with her tongue twirled the cigarette around into her mouth so I couldn't see it.

Her name was Catalina and we saw her several times and tried to invite her to our Bible studies after they got started. She came once or twice, but when her husband Val nearly sliced his heal off in a motorcycle accident, she brought him into town to the church to see "Doc" Lhey. The wound looked bad. It was all black and swollen. Lhey took them to the same hospital where she had taken Violeta when we first started. They had always given us good service there in the past, but this time the doctor looked at his foot and without even examining it said very brusquely that he would have to be admitted to the hospital for surgery. Lhey was fit to be tied by the doctor's rude attitude and lack of real concern so she brought them back to the church.

We got out the peroxide and ointment, some soap and soft cloths, and Doc Lhey went to work. The first problem was that since he'd had the wound it had never been cleaned. It was black due to dirt. Lhey very carefully washed the dirt away and then using a sterilized knife cut the infection to drain the pus out. After cleaning it out we could see that it was a deep cut, but not serious if just treated. The doctor at the hospital was likely going to amputate his foot, but Lhey's tender care led to a full recovery. She put on ointment and a bandage, gave them extra bandages and told them to change the wrap every day.

Then Lhey sat down with Val and Catalina and began to share the gospel with them. The tricycle driver that had brought them all the way from Pastolan was sitting by and I invited him to join them. Lhey likes to present the gospel using red and black pens to illustrate the heart condition and the cross. When she sits down with people to explain salvation they usually don't get away. The Lord has blessed her with an exceptional ability in the area of soul winning. In a little while all three of them had prayed with her to be saved, and Val and Catalina never missed another Bible study until we left on furlough.

Des, the councilwoman who had showed us around on our second visit to Pastolan came to a couple of Bible studies but afterward we rarely saw her. We hadn't seen her husband, Pablo, at the gate for some time. Then one day visiting in the village we came to their house. Pablo was sitting in a chair by the door, but only when we came up to him did we notice the bandage on the end of his leg. His right foot and ankle had been amputated due to complications from diabetes. We asked them how he was getting around and they said they borrowed a wheelchair from someone up the hill when they needed, but he was unable to get out much. They were beginning to get desperate because he had no more work. After we visited a while Lhey began to share the gospel with them and they prayed with her to be saved.

Lhey and I discussed it later and decided we needed to try and get them a wheelchair. I sent out an email mentioning the need and a friend of ours in Florida, Bud Trill, responded by sending the money for the purchase of a wheelchair. Pablo and Des had not asked for help and when we brought it a couple weeks later they were so thankful they broke down in tears. With Pablo mobile, Des pushed him up the hill to our Bible studies every week after that.

We had previously acquired a wheelchair for another family with a boy named Emboy who was crippled from the waist down. Danny and Rose lived just below our meeting place on the slope in a small house. It consisted of a sleeping area off the ground about six feet wide and twelve feet in length. The corners were anchored with poles and the walls and floor were made of bamboo. They had a porch area where they cooked about the same size as the sleeping area but with no floor and it was all covered with large sections of canvass.

When they first started coming to the Bible studies Danny carried Emboy up the hill to our pavilion. His legs were stiff and sometimes spastic with one foot slightly clubbed. Emboy was eleven years old and seemed to be bright, but he had never been in school. His elbows were heavily calloused from crawling around and black from the dirt.

Rose told us one day that Emboy had said he wished he could just die because his life was boring and meaningless. We thought a wheelchair might give him a better outlook so we arranged to purchase one. Then Lhey gave them money to bring Emboy to the church in town. They got a tricycle and Rose brought Emboy along with his two sisters.

They were overwhelmed when they saw the wheelchair. Emboy didn't want to go home. "I want to see the world," he said, and so they strolled around the streets of town so he could soak it all in. Imagine a boy who in eleven years had never left the jungle and was seeing buildings, roads, and other people for the first time. When he got hungry Lhey gave him another treat; his first McDonald's hamburger.

Rarely have I ever seen someone so grateful. At the next Bible study Rose wheeled Emboy up a narrow trail through the woods to our meeting. He wanted to sit with the children in their class, but first he asked if he could tell us thank you. So we wheeled him in front and he sang us a song that he made up just to tell us how thankful he was. The sheer joy on his face and the tears in his parent's eyes are some of the things that make it all worthwhile.

I was concerned how they would get him through the jungle to the house because it is just a little foot trail through the trees, but Danny and Rose weren't at all worried. They push, pull, lift, and struggle over tree roots, stones and the rough path without complaint. They are happy to have the wheelchair.

Still, there were more medical needs than we could handle on our own so when I heard about Bethany Bible Baptist, a very large church in Manila that sponsors medical mission teams several times each year, I contacted them to see if we could schedule them in Pastolan. They agreed and we talked with Condrado, the chieftain, and he agreed to let them come in March 2015. The elementary school had just had its graduation and they had built a bamboo pole palm branch covered pavilion over the outdoor basketball court the week before. We asked if they would leave that up for us and we used it as an admittance, triage and witnessing area. Doctors and dentists used several of the school classrooms to treat minor cases.

The team arrived at the church early on a Saturday morning in six vehicles. There were about thirty people plus their supplies of medicines. We provided breakfast and then our ladies fixed spaghetti that we took up to the village for their lunch later on. We also had a dentist in our church and the eye doctor, Marvin Azuscena, who offered to help. Doc Marvin checked the eyes and donated pairs of glasses for over forty people. By the end of the day the team had treated 364 people with over a hundred salvation decisions in the counseling sessions.

The clinic was open to the entire village and many people we had not met before came as well as the folks we had been working with. Sometimes you wonder, especially when there are language barriers, if you are really communicating and getting through to people. The director of the team told us afterward that they were surprised how many people that they tried to share the gospel with already knew and were confident in their salvation. When we asked who they were we found they were the people we had been working with. Obviously we were connecting and they were understanding.

Chapter Fourteen
Suffer the Little Children

These words of Jesus in Matthew 19:14, "Suffer the little children to come unto me," means to "Allow" the little children. Children's ministries are vital to any mission or church work. Most of the salvation decisions made will be by children and teenagers, thus the importance of a good youth program reaching the children before they get hardened by the world.

At FOFBC we had a Christian kindergarten for children ages four to five. We were unable to grow any larger due to regulations regarding the size of our lot and facilities. The most students we ever had in a single year was twenty-two, but they came from all backgrounds in the neighborhood: Catholics, Jehovah's Witnesses and even *Iglesia Ni Cristo*, a cult church that denies the deity of Christ. It opened many opportunities to get the gospel into these homes.

As part of our regular church programs we had children's Bible clubs in three different areas of town. One of these was in a place called Little Baguio. Baguio is a resort town in the mountains a hundred miles to the north located at an elevation of five thousand feet. The roads up are steep and twisting. Little Baguio is a squatter area built up on the sides of one of the hills surrounding Olongapo. Olongapo sits in kind of a bowl with high ridges around the city on three sides with the southwest side resting on the bay.

On the east side of the town the ridge is almost straight up, but enterprising people built homes on the slopes and an entire community with a school and *barangay* center are hidden up in the trees above the town. There are two ways up to the community. The long way starts by the main road where it leaves town and is a very long gradual walk up the hillside.

The other, which is closer and quicker to reach from the church, goes up a very steep concrete stairway. There are 216 mostly uneven steps, some wide, some narrow, most about twelve to fifteen inches up, but many as high as eighteen inches and even higher stepping up. One of our church members lives up there in a nice house overlooking the cliff about 300 feet above the city below. It is a challenge in the heat to go up, but several of our church young people make the trip each Saturday to hold a Bible club.

Every year during the school vacation time we also hold a Daily Vacation Bible School at the church for the neighborhood kids in the mornings, and at the outreaches in the afternoons. A lot of children whom we would not be able to get down to the church every Sunday have heard the gospel through these programs and responded.

At Pastolan we began teaching the Christian Religious Education class on Mondays. It was soon clear to us that many of the children didn't get lunch, so we began bringing snacks for the kids to eat on each visit.

The rainy season had also just started when we began going up to teach. The first time a storm broke out while we were there we noticed that only a handful of the kids had umbrellas. Most would take a sheet of plastic or a large garbage bag and put their head through a hole in the middle to wear it like a poncho. Others just held the plastic over their heads.

We decided one of the things we could do would be to provide umbrellas for the kids. We found small, children size umbrellas at the mall in town for only $2.50 each. It's not much, we thought, but when we started buying for 250 kids that suddenly came out to $625. Still, we saw it as a way to build a rapport with the kids so we bought them and brought them up to the school. The kids were so happy that the school took pictures of them to give to us. Unfortunately they all had their umbrellas opened so when we got the photos we could barely see any of their faces. But it accomplished our purpose.

We started with Lhey, our church Bible woman, Perl, Lhey's cousin, Sharon, the youth pastor, Javis, and whomever he would bring to help him. We only had an hour and not enough people to engage every class that long, so we divided into groups. There were eight classes total when we first went, one for each grade with two third grade sections and a kindergarten.

Lhey and the girls would start with the first grade while Javis and his rotating assistants would go to the second. Each week they would swap around. While they were teaching the little kids I engaged the third graders going back and forth from each class teaching them memory verses and songs. After fifteen minutes when the teachers came to the third grade I moved on to the fourth and fifth grades. In another fifteen minutes when they moved up again I went to the sixth grade, and last Lhey would go to the kindergarten kids.

We were limited on time but our system got us around each week and the kids for the most part were pretty cooperative. One thing that surprised me was the seeming lack of interest of the teachers. I would have expected them to sit in their classrooms to help keep the kids in order while we taught. No such thing. As soon as we arrived they departed. Except for the third graders most of the kids were pretty well behaved, but there were times when you could feel a storm coming by their edginess.

The sixth graders were much more proficient in English and they enjoyed my stumbling around trying to tell Bible stories in Tagalog. I used a mixture of English and Tagalog known as *Taglish*. These kids had very little knowledge of the Bible. Even the very popular story of David and Goliath was foreign to them. I started teaching them from the creation in Genesis and taught my way through the Old Testament to get to Christ and finally the Romans Road.

The story of Abraham and Isaac illustrates how lacking in biblical knowledge they were. The children all thought it was funny that Abraham and Sarah were so old and still having children. None of them had heard the story before. When I told of God telling Abraham to sacrifice Isaac, the look of horror that came on their faces was stunning.

I had some poster size pictures to use as aids to tell the story and when I got to Abraham taking the knife I raised my hand in the air and just as I started to bring it down I shouted, "*Wag!*" Don't! Some of them were half standing in their seats and suddenly they clutched their chests and sat down with a big sigh and a smile. The look of relief on their faces was priceless, but I couldn't believe their reaction. I finished the story relating how Jesus was the sacrificial Lamb that God would provide and they seemed to understand the picture.

I felt like I was connecting and developing a rapport with the kids when one day some of them said to me, "Pastolan plus Pastor Lance equals *Pastolance*." By the end of our first year of teaching most of the older kids had prayed with us to be saved.

We had a very active youth department at FOFBC. Some of the young people stemmed from an AWANA program we started at the church in 2005. Behind the church a couple blocks away was a football stadium and track with a basketball court on the side and a swimming pool. It was called the "Oval" and backed up to an elementary school on the far side.

A great many kids from the area had been saved including a group that called themselves the "Bacon Street Gang" for the street they lived on. Six of them had either attended or graduated from Bible college, and one young man named Javis did his internship with us and the church hired him as our youth pastor and song leader.

All of them were active in the church and helped with our Vacation Bible School programs. Younger kids also joined in following their examples. VBS was a big production every year and all these kids volunteered to help. It was a blessing to see their enthusiasm for the Lord. We planned to take the VBS program up to Pastolan and when we presented the idea to our youth they enthusiastically volunteered to help. Lhey and the ladies at the church prepared snacks, sandwiches and chicken stew to bring for the kids, and then fixed lunch for all the helpers. My role in it all became just ferrying the kids, supplies and food up to the village while they held the same program for the *Aeta* kids as they held for the kids in town.

We had twenty workers go up with us in 2015 to hold a three-day abbreviated version of the program we used at the church and had seventy-five kids attend. Nineteen were saved. The next year we had twenty-two helpers and had eighty-two kids on the first day, but we were disappointed because we were expecting a lot more.

I walked down through the village to see if I could round up some kids but the ones I found wouldn't come. When I arrived at Marilyn's house she told a boy to go with me but he said no because he was afraid he would get shot. After a little discussion I figured out that he meant to say, "to get a shot." No, I told him, we are not the medical people.

Baby boys in the Philippines are not normally circumcised at birth. Many families will have it taken care of later, but for the indigent native people like the *Aetas* the government has a free program for their male children. Unfortunately, the next day a government medical team was coming to give the free circumcisions. It all but killed our VBS program, as the next two days there were no boys attending.

Ethan was our very late blessing. I was already fifty-three when he was born, but he has kept me young. Lhey was ten years younger but still getting along for having a baby. Lhey and I couldn't have asked for a better gift. He seems to have a knack for languages. He was three years old when we left Kenya, but playing in the yard every day with our guard's children he was already picking up Swahili and interacting with them. He was five when we arrived back in the Philippines. The first two months we stayed with Lhey's *Tiyay* (aunt) Wilma and her cousins Toto and Fen. Their son David was just a year older than Ethan but the same size and they played together with the neighborhood children. In only a couple of weeks I noticed Ethan was picking up Tagalog, and in six weeks he was speaking it fluently.

The Filipino school year had already started but we enrolled him in a kindergarten class at a private school, Brightfields Academy, which used a Montessori curriculum. It was an advanced level program and we got him into school just one week before the semester break. They had two weeks off and Lhey spent almost every waking moment with him studying to get him caught up. He learned it quickly and by the end of the school year he had the highest grades in his class.

In the first grade he competed all year with a girl named Angel. Filipinos are big on pageantry and in the schools they go overboard with beauty contests attempting to train even the youngest of children how to model. Ethan's school held a pageant to elect a king and queen as well as a prince and princess. The king and queen were chosen from the high school level, and the prince and princess from the elementary. Ethan and Angel won. They were dressed in golden royal garb and crowns and a parade was held through the city streets with them sitting on large chairs in the bed of a pickup truck decorated like a throne room. Angel finished first in academics that year and Ethan was second.

At the end of the school year Ethan was asked to pose for an advertising poster for the school. At the same time a flyer advertising a modeling contest was posted at the school and many of Ethan's classmates were signing up. Ethan wanted to join them, and thinking it would be some simple activity we signed him up.

It turned out not to be a simple activity. A major modeling company from Manila called *Ystilo* was hosting it. There were different levels of competition for the different age groups and hundreds of kids had signed up. Ethan competed in the age five to nine level. We had to sign a statement that we would not pull Ethan out of the event early and for several weeks he had rehearsals and photo shoots preparing for the big show to be held in a three-story high exhibition center of the Ayala Mall on SBMA.

The big night came and the mall was jammed with hundreds of people. There was a general parade of all the models and then each group had to model a white suit, a black suit, and some casual wear. Ethan was the first out for his age group wearing the white suit. He came across the stage from the left and when he reached the runway he slid his left foot out, turned to face the judges at the end of the ramp, and then slid his right foot up putting his left hand on his hip. He was a natural. When he slid his foot and turned all the teenie-boppers in the audience cheered and screamed. Then he walked down to the judges, calmly looked them all in the eyes, and then turned to go back. He was unbelievable.

When it was over he won all the awards for his age group but two. He was standing on the walkway with the winners from the other categories with two trophies, several framed certificates and ribbons, and two large posters mounted on Styrofoam backing. He couldn't even hold it all, so I went up to collect it from him.

I have no doubt the experience did wonders for his personal esteem and self-confidence, but when it was over we decided it was the end of his modeling career. Lhey was with him at every rehearsal and photo shoot, watching closely everything that was done because half the staff and trainers were gay and transgenders. He'd had enough exposure to it and we didn't think he needed anymore.

The best thing to come out of it all was that Ethan remained the same gentle, caring, precious child that he had always been. It didn't go to his head. There was one little boy in his group named Hanz who was only five-years-old. When we saw Hanz with his mother and went to greet them after the contest Hanz was crying because he hadn't won any awards. Ethan put his hand on his shoulder and said, "It's okay. Here, you can have one of mine."

We weren't through with the pageantry yet. The next December there was an ad for a singing contest called Voice Kids. It was set up somewhat like the American Idol program and all the kids at Ethan's school were joining, so we signed him up. He did well. They competed at several different locations around town, but the final was at the mall.

Ethan qualified for the contest singing "You Know Better Than I," and in front of the hundreds at the mall he sang "You Raise Me Up" for the final. Out of a hundred that passed the initial audition, he came in fifth place, which was a fair finish I thought. There were some kids with unbelievable voices for eight and nine year olds but we were very proud of Ethan.

I share this to point out that Ethan quickly fit in, got involved in activities at the church, and easily built a rapport with his Filipino friends. Our oldest son, Jonathan, also easily fit in with the kids his age when we were in the Philippines for short periods of time. But he grew up in Kenya. He easily made friends with the Kenyan kids at our churches, but where we lived there were only a few kids that came by to play with him and after the first few months when the novelty of the white kid in the neighborhood wore off they never came around. We lived an hour from his school and he never had the opportunities that Ethan had.

It's one of the burdens missionary parents carry. Am I doing the right thing for my child? There were many advantages to growing up in Kenya, but Jonathan was a very sociable, people person, and missed out on many of the things his classmates who lived closer to their school got to do. And as I became more involved in the work and some of the struggles, spending three hours a day in the car driving Jonathan to and from school and out to the college and back, I was often too tired to spend the time with him he needed. Other times when the pressures of the work would build up I would get short-tempered and wind up taking it out unfairly on Jonathan.

And then when he was only thirteen, his best friend, Gully, whom he had loved like a brother, was taken away from him in death. I wasn't quick enough to realize it until later, but it had to have been a difficult existence for Jonathan in many ways, and my heart breaks thinking about it. Still, he never gave us any trouble, was always involved in the work, and turned out to be a fine young gentleman of whom we are very proud.

When Ethan was seven years old the Vacation Bible School theme song at FOFBC that year was "He Knows My Name." Ethan's class sang it for the parents in the graduation ceremony on Saturday. The song impressed me so much that I asked them to sing it again the next day in church and I preached on it.

I have a Maker, He formed my heart.
Before even time began my life was in His hands.
He knows my name; He knows my every thought;
He sees each tear that falls, and hears me when I call.

I have a Father, He calls me His own.
He'll never leave me no matter where I go.
He knows my name; He knows my every thought;
He sees each tear that falls, and hears me when I call.

God knew me before I was born, and He loved me in spite of who I am, what I've done, or what privileges I've been blessed with. But He also knows the *Aeta* children, dirt poor, living in falling down bamboo houses, covered with sores, suffering from malnutrition, all but forgotten by the world, and He loves them. On a world stage they may be an insignificant people, but on God's stage they are as important as the President of the United States.

Chapter Fifteen
A Special Guest

First Olongapo Fundamental Baptist Church was founded in 1975. I first became connected with the church when I arrived in the Philippines in the Navy in 1985. I met Lhey in the church and we were married in 1991. In 2005 we came over from Kenya to help the church for a year. Then in 2013 we came back to the Philippines and the church asked if I would accept the position as their pastor.

In January 2015 the church celebrated its fortieth anniversary. By then I had been associated with the church off and on for thirty years. The members wanted to make the fortieth a landmark celebration. We kicked it off with a big day at the church on the actual anniversary date the third Sunday of January, but then extended it all the way until the end of May. I invited in to speak as many former pastors and seminary students who had gone out from our church and were pastoring churches as I could contact. Some former members who were living in the States also came over to take part.

In March we held a weeklong mission conference inviting four new Filipino missionaries going through the Asian Baptist Clearing House to present their works. One was in China, one in Vietnam, one was going to Argentina and one to Mozambique. I introduced the church to the concept of Faith Promise missions giving. The people embraced the principle, gave willingly, and we were able to support all four missionaries and over the next two years we added two more.

The events concluded at the end of May with a Bible conference that included three former pastors and three Bible college students out of our church as speakers and I gave a soul-winning seminar. The conference ran from Thursday to Sunday with a guest keynote speaker from the States who spoke each night, Dr. Les Heinze from Red Rocks Baptist Church, our sending church in Morrison, Colorado.

In Pastolan our Bible study in front of Fletcher's house had grown and we moved around behind his house where there was less noise from the road and several logs on the ground that could be used for benches. As our numbers grew and we began to have seventy or eighty each week that area became too small.

The folks knew so little about the Bible that we kept the lessons as simple as possible in the beginning, but we were all meeting together, adults, children and babies. One afternoon we had to contend with a large *carabao* (a very docile water buffalo) that a neighbor had tied to a tree right next to us and reminded us of his presence with an occasional "moo." Chickens also ran around, some even climbing up slanted tree trunks into the branches above.

We began to talk about a larger area to meet. Fletcher volunteered another spot a little further back into the trees but it was too crowded by the forest. Then Mario's daughter, Irene, offered to let us use her place. She lived on one of the last plots in the village at the top of the mountain. Her husband, Johnny Tupaz, was a carpenter of sorts and was building them the only two-story house in the village. But they claimed a large area of land and offered to let us build next to their house in a cleared space.

We staked out a spot 20 x 20 and I paid Johnny to gather the materials needed. When the tribal council heard what we were doing some were upset that we were going to try to take their land. We explained to them that we were only putting up a temporary shelter, and that if we ever leave we will give it to Johnny and Irene. They decided it was okay and we proceeded to build. We used log posts with a full wall of bamboo nipa in the back and half walls on the sides with the front open and a tin roof. Johnny built the building and even built benches using bamboo slats.

We had a decent assembly area with places to sit for the adults, and we had room for the kids to meet under the trees on the other side of Irene's house. Then several people at FOFBC started volunteering to go along with us. Soon we had eight to ten helpers going with us each week. They helped to divide the children into primaries, juniors and teenage groups.

The pavilion was ready just after Christmas and we moved up the hill. With the new meeting place, the space and divided classes our attendance began to grow from around seventy-five to over one hundred twenty. It was just at the end of the typhoon season and there had been very few tourists at Pamulaklakin. Many of the people were out of work, had no money, and were hungry, some even showing signs of malnutrition. We always tried to have a bottle of vitamins to give to people, and then we started making sandwiches and cookies for snacks after the Bible study. On special occasions we would prepare a large cooking pot of rice and of chicken stew.

For our church anniversary in January we had invited some other churches to join us including our daughter church in the Roosevelt district that FOFBC had started in 1991. We also invited the *Aeta* to come. I told Fletcher that I couldn't go up to get them, but if they could get to the church I would pay for their transport. He came with twenty-four. We set a church attendance record of 301.

We had a partially potluck, partially catered lunch for everyone, but we had to borrow tables and chairs from the City Hall to seat everyone. The Olongapo city government offers tables, chairs and tents free of charge for churches to use for activities. We had the chairs arranged around the tables, of course, but the *Aeta* folks were funny. They set their plates on the chairs and used them as tables and knelt on the ground to eat.

At the beginning of January 2015 SBMA had widened the trail from Pamulaklakin into a narrow one-lane road up to Pastolan. It was still rough, rocky and steep, and not conducive to small cars. We had to rent an SUV to make the drive. It was only three kilometers from Pamulaklakin to the village and cut the time by two-thirds getting there from FOFBC as compared with going through Tipo town on the paved road.

In 2016 they widened and graded the road again until it was smooth enough for a compact car to go over. They also paved the road up passed Irene's house in the village so that it wasn't quite as dusty at our meeting place when the occasional vehicle went by. When the rains came, however, it washed out the shortcut road and nothing could pass over the mud. Then after a long dry season there were places on the road that were so thick with dust that they were almost as slippery as snow. Tires had a hard time getting traction.

By March 2015 it had been a year since I found Fletcher and we had been meeting regularly with the *Aetas* for nearly nine months. We had close to a hundred adults and teens that had made professions of faith who were faithfully attending the Bible studies. We began teaching about baptism and preparing them to have a baptismal service. Most of them readily accepted the idea, but there were many questions. My concern was that they truly understood what baptism was about and not thinking it was a part of their salvation, but a testimony of their already having received Christ as Savior.

I went to Pamulaklakin one day with Fletcher and Irene to find a suitable spot along the river to baptize. The river down the hill behind the kiosks was either too deep or too shallow, so we went around the bend to the other side of the hill and there was a wide-open spot and a section of the river just under waist deep for me.

We planned it for the Saturday during the Bible conference when Les Heinze was going to be there. It would be the final event before the final service of our extended anniversary. The ladies at the church went to work planning and preparing food for the occasion. We were finally ready.

Les Heinze's flight came in to Manila at midnight on Tuesday. I took James with me to pick him up. The midnight flights are usually the best. The city is gone to bed, there are very few vehicles out and we made the trip from the airport to Olongapo in just over two hours where normally it takes up to four hours during the day.

Our Bible conference began Thursday afternoon. We had three speakers, a break, then I held a soul-winning seminar, then we had dinner, and Pastor Heinze spoke for the evening session. Friday was the same and we had a good turnout of our people each day.

On Saturday we had our Aeta baptism in the river at Pamulaklakin. Sixty of the *Aeta* folks came down from the mountain, and others were around but they had to work as they had a lot of tourists that day. We also had fifty-seven folks from church come out to join us for the baptism, followed by a baby dedication, and then an *Aeta* picnic with bamboo cooked rice and chicken. We also brought a lot of electric rice cooker prepared rice because the *Aetas* like that better than the bamboo prepared rice that they make.

We had been praying that the Lord would hold back the rain. Rainy season officially begins June 1, but that Saturday was only two days early, and we'd had a few light showers over the previous couple of weeks. It was hot when we arrived in Pamulaklakin, but when I drove up to get Mario and Violeta who were too weak to make the trip down on foot, some really dark clouds rolled in and I began to pray for the Lord to hold back the storm. We eventually had a light sprinkle by the river, but it poured up at Pastolan. When I drove some of the folks back up afterward some of the long steep sections of the road were muddy and we slipped and slid a couple times, but I had a Toyota SUV that day and we made it.

I had Dr. Heinze explain baptism one more time with James translating to make certain everyone understood what we were doing. Then I went down into the water and found a good location.

I baptized thirty-four that day, the most I'd ever done at one service. We had more signed up, but it turned out to be a big day at the resort with a lot of visitors needing tour guides in the jungle, so some of our folks were unable to make it. The worst part was keeping my balance in the river because I was on a slight slope and the water was flowing slowly, but I braced my right foot against a big rock and it worked. Except for two larger people, most of them probably didn't weigh more than eighty or eighty-five pounds so it didn't wear me out too much.

Only one person panicked and swallowed water, but I had a hard time getting four or five of them to understand they had to hold their nose when they went under. Julio, who had been bitten by a snake in the jungle only three weeks before, had recovered, and he made the most unusual exit from a "baptistry" I've ever seen. When I raised him back up from the water he dived forward and swam under the surface to the other side of the river. I couldn't stop laughing and neither could the folks on the bank watching.

From the time I had first mentioned baptism Fletcher had come forward and took the lead encouraging the people to be baptized. His influence helped several who seemed to be shy about stepping out to make the decision as well. Fletcher led by example. He told me several times, "I will be the first," and he was.

Chapter Sixteen
The People We Love

Aeta young people face the same cares and temptations that all youth do. In a culture with few sexual mores, where marriage is simply a couple moving in together with no serious thought of fidelity, there are many teenage girls who wind up pregnant with no man to take care of them. One fourteen-year-old girl became so distraught over breaking up with a boyfriend that she committed suicide.

Another teen was brutally murdered one night. Her body was found a week later by a worker in the forest, hung up in a tree and gutted like a deer. Police quickly descended on the village and arrested four men who had been working on a solar panel project on the next mountain. They confessed that they had been drunk and carried out the deed. What really struck us, however, was that the girl had been missing for several days and her parents had never reported it. She apparently had run away before and they just figured she was running around with friends and saw no need.

We hadn't met these girls, but we were soon faced with death among the folks we were working with. Pilita had been saved at our Bible studies and asked us to visit her husband, Julian. They lived far back in the jungle. He had severe intestinal problems and bleeding. When we took him to the government hospital they immediately wanted to do surgery for what they said was a giant tumor in his colon. They hadn't done any tests and Lhey was upset. She asked them if they had ever considered he might have worms. They finally did a test and found he had a ball of worms at the end of his colon. Worm medicine cleared him out and for a while he improved and came to our Bible studies.

Julian eventually trusted the Lord, but his intestinal problems continued and his condition slowly deteriorated until one day we got the word he had died. He was only in his forties. Friends ran extension cords all the way out to his house so they could have light for the wake and we went up two nights to hold a service. The next day we buried him in a small vault above ground at the cemetery behind the elementary school.

In January 2017 Mario, who had just turned eighty, became so weak he could no longer come up the hill to the Bible studies. In fact he hardly ever left his bed. We often went down to his house to visit and pray with him and Violeta after the Bible studies and brought him food and medicine, but his condition didn't improve and three months later he passed away. We held services each night at the home of one of his sons that lived on the left side of the Y intersection in the village. The family was stoic, as always, card games would go on before we came and after we left as they sat up with the body through the night.

The day of the burial, however, we were surprised at the reaction of Violeta and many of the grandchildren. When we brought the coffin out to the hearse, a pickup truck, Violeta began wailing and screaming and the young girls followed her lead. She almost had to be carried by two people, one on either side, up the trail to the cemetery, but the worst came when they began to seal up the vault. She threw herself over the coffin, screaming, as did the girls. Irene, also crying, held her mother and tried to comfort her, but it seemed for Violeta there was no help.

We began to realize that the concept of eternal security and a reunion in heaven had not sunk in. Irene had understood but Violeta had not. Violeta next asked us if we would go with her on the fortieth day after Mario's death to pray for him. It's a tradition that comes from Catholic influence, but is somewhat similar to what we faced when Ezekiel died in Kenya.

Lhey explained to her again that there was no need since Mario was already in heaven and as they were talking the light came on in Violeta's eyes and tears of joy ran down her cheeks. In the *Aeta* culture there was no hope for the future, and the few who had been exposed to Catholicism had only the thought of purgatory and punishment, but no assurance of a happy day ahead.

Holy Week is a big event in the predominantly Catholic Philippines. Every year on Good Friday penitents begin walking the streets; young men flagellate themselves with quirts with razor blades tied into the strips until their backs are ripped open and bleeding, old women walk the streets with heavy burdens on their shoulders and barefoot until their feet bleed. On the highway near our house young men wearing no shirts lay flat on the hot pavement before taking up a heavy cross and carrying it a half mile up the road to a Catholic church to take communion. Pretend mockers will follow throwing sticks at them while helpers are standing by with water when they collapse. An hour away in San Fernando there are some so devout that they volunteer to be crucified and held up before a crowd for several minutes before being taken down.

And all for naught. You can't argue with their sincerity or devotion, but salvation or approval from God is not found in self-sacrifice or good works. It is found in faith in Jesus Christ and His completed work on the cross at Calvary (Ephesians 2:8-9). In an attempt to offer people the biblical way we held a Seven Last Sayings service at FOFBC each Good Friday. We followed it with a sunrise service at the beach on Sunday morning. The message of the cross only begins with the crucifixion. It is completed with the resurrection of the Lord.

The Catholics come and hold a mass from time to time in Pastolan, but we haven't seen any of the penitent type of activity taking place in the village. Rather, every year at Easter the *Aetas* make a traditional trek several miles to their original homeland at Boton. They go there to camp out and live off the land, hunting *bayawak* (monitor lizard) and fishing in the river and the bay. As a result we never had a Bible study at Easter in the village. Nearly everyone is gone.

We felt especially blessed when in 2016 the folks in our Bible study invited us to visit them. We found them under a bridge over the river and then hiked way back into the woods where one group was camping out. They were sleeping on hammocks or blankets over cardboard under the trees. One girl had cut her foot so we brought bandages and antibiotics for her. We also brought a couple of chickens and they provided clams and fish. After eating they loaded us down with clams and oysters to take home.

We had come to feel like the *Aeta* folks were part of our own family, and I believe they felt the same about us. One day as I was visiting with some men in the village one of them said to me, "Oh, you are Fletcher's best friend." When Pastor James Dequina made a video of the *Aetas,* to give to us as we were departing for furlough he interviewed Fletcher, and Fletcher made the comment, "Pastor Lance and I are best friends."

We had been in the Philippines four years. It had been over three years since we first made our way to Pastolan and found Fletcher. It was time for us to go home on furlough. When I first mentioned to our Bible study that we would be leaving the people almost panicked. "Are you coming back?" they all wanted to know. "*O-o*," I told them. Yes. We would be gone for a year to report to our churches and supporters. I needed to raise some funds so we could build a permanent building when we got back.

"But you are sure you will come back?" They were worried. I tried to reassure them. "*Babalik kami,*" I said. We shall return. "Pastor James will look in on you when he is able," I told them.

We prepared a meal for everyone on our last visit. One hundred twenty-four attended and many of the ladies cried as they hugged Lhey and begged her over and over not to forget them.

In June 2017 we came home to the States and I began traveling to our supporting churches to report on our work in the Philippines. Then three weeks before Christmas we got word that Pablo had died. The thought came to me, What if we hadn't gone? What if people hadn't given and churches hadn't sent so that we could take the gospel to needy people who have never heard?

We will not forget the *Aetas.* We have never forgotten them. Since we first met them in 1992 after digging out from the Mt. Pinatubo eruption, the name of Fletcher Abraham has been on my prayer list. The children on the bench in the jungle listening to Bible stories for the first time have been in our hearts. Now that we have found Fletcher and his family, the children grown, the grandchildren, and their village, it is our desire to return and continue to share the love of Christ with the *Aeta* people whom we also have come to love.

A ten-minute video of the *Aeta* ministry can be found on Youtube under "Patterson Furlough Video 2017."
https://youtu.be/-L_jnKq6rMA

If you wish to contribute to the *Aeta* work please send to:
Lance Patterson
Baptist Bible Fellowship, Int.
Box 191
Springfield, MO 65801
417-862-5001
Personal contact: pattersonlance@yahoo.com

94728692R00078

Made in the USA
Columbia, SC
04 May 2018